No Axe
Too Small to Grind

No Axe
Too Small to Grind

—— The Best of ——
JOEY SLINGER

McClelland and Stewart

McClelland and Stewart Limited
The Canadian Publishers
Toronto, Ontario
M4B 3G2

Canadian Cataloguing in Publication Data

Slinger, Joey.
   No axe too small to grind

A selection of the author's columns from the
Toronto Star.
ISBN 0-7710-8206-1

I. The Toronto Star. I. Title.

PS8587.L56N6 1985   O81   C85-099212-5
PR9199.3.S55N6 1985

Printed and bound in Canada by John Deyell Company

Contents

My reign as Miss Canada
Our deadly bread
Dental hygiene is moral hygiene
Depravity of the week
Talking turkey
The wild raspberry caper

3. *Arts and Litter* / 52

Country and Proust
Mr. Bone and the fossil hunters
The snows of Hemingway
T for two
J.D. is a pest
Send no money
Morning men
The great art doors
Is Mick Jagger smart?
Waiting for Waterloo
Following the leaves

4. *Sports Snorts* / 72

Off my game
Talk it up
Icing the old folks
The skater
Bag-lady baseball
Spitting it out
Hat tricks
Baseball jargon
Hawks, a golden eagle, a golden afternoon

5. *Painless Politics* / 89

Options
Open to hostilities

Playing for laughs
Shadow of the cruise
Following the leader
Feeling at home
Politics makes strange dead fellows
To thine own self be false
As the Crow passes
Singing the greys

6. *Above the Crowd* / 108

Love that Larry
Giving Daniel credit
Terry passes
There went Santa Claus
Ah, Cisco!
The coal mine's ghosts
Longevity is reward of dissolute
Amicus
A grump afoot

7. *T. O.* / 125

Positively Orwellian
Fixing the old place up
The Rosedale bus
Wild bicycles
A walk on the mild side
Nothing finer than Spadina
Wall of love
Landmarks to go
Hi, sailor!
Glorious slush

8. *Write-Offs* / 144

My first novel

Sex and scandal
Grammar, safe and easy
How to write
The $1.5 million write-off
Upper Volta gets a jolt
Call our toll-free numbers
Gun news, balloon news
The flower bomb

9. Personals / 161

10. Life's Not Like That / 184

For Jake and Lucy

Preface

This book was commissioned as a *Guide to Moral Fitness* and was
to be illustrated with actual photographs of the author in a leotard
doing the exercises he undertakes daily to improve his rectitude and
tone up principles that have run to fat, but that idea got lost somewhere along the way. I don't know where. I might have left it on the
subway. It's too bad, because it would have been a dandy book – just
looking at the photographs makes me break out in an idealistic
sweat, and I imagine the text would have been equally inspirational.
That's how it is with a book, though. When you start off you never
know what's going to become of it. It's all right for a reader. A reader
can read the reviews and say, "Ah, so that's what this book is about,"
and know exactly what he's getting into, but the author doesn't have
reviews to go by when he's writing. Every word he sets down is a step
into the unknown. It's a foolish way to operate, when you think
about it, like building a house and then pulling out the blueprint to
see if what you ended up with bears any resemblance to what it was
supposed to be. Book writing will never be on a solid footing until
reviews are published first and given to authors who can then turn
out their books accordingly. If there is ever a royal commission into
book writing, and we're certainly due for one, that's what I will
recommend.

With the *Guide to Moral Fitness* gone by the boards, the book
then became a novel about a young boy growing up in a Fine Old

Ontario Family, and his quest to become an ethnic. It was a block-buster set against the sweeping panorama of the Battle of Jenkin's Ear and would have been a sure-fire bestseller if it had contained a plot and characters. But time was running out and there was no money in the kitty for a plot and characters. All we could afford was punctuation, and while some of it was first-rate, the publisher believed that an historical novel with an ethnic twist about the United Empire Loyalists that consisted only of punctuation was leaving too much to chance. People could read God knows what into it.

After that, the book was, briefly, a script for a television series on compost, a recipe for Veal Supreme, a sonnet cycle glorifying dairy price supports, and a home auto-repair manual. None of these was found to be satisfactory, especially the recipe for Veal Supreme, which, for some reason no one can figure out, called for six gallons of 4 Aces Sherry, a box of Alpha-Bits, and included the home address of Evelyn Kostelnyk in Estevan, Saskatchewan, who, it turns out, moved to North Battleford years ago. When she got married. It tasted dreadful.

All further plans had to be abandoned when the deadline ceased looming and roared through like a hurricane, leaving a trail of car-nage and shattered dreams. It was all the survivors could do to assemble a collection of short pieces that had previously been pub-lished in *The Toronto Star*, although the newspaper denies it and will punch you in the nose if you press the point.

A word about facts: the facts in this book shouldn't be taken too literally, unless they happen to be accurate. And I have discovered, too late, it turns out, to do anything about it, that some people find some of these pieces humorous. That bothers me. There is nothing worse than writing a thoughtful piece about the perils besetting man-kind and to discover someone laughing. What's so funny about the Organization of Petroleum Exporting Countries? Or the fact that Niagara Falls has jelled? If I have written anything funny about stuff like that, I'm sorry. I didn't know I was doing it. It is unconscious humour. Unconscious humour is the worst kind because you don't know it's happening and your inclination is to suggest that whoever is laughing seek professional counselling. Unconscious humour is not to be confused with unintentional humour. Unintentional humour is when you're writing about another Russian wheat-crop failure and what comes out is about the Baptist with the wooden leg who met the nun with the chainsaw. You didn't intend for that to come out, it just came out. Don't go looking for anything like that here.

Listen, what I'm trying to get at is this: none of this stuff is supposed to be humorous. This is a serious book covering a full range of serious topics. If you want to laugh, fine. But it's your funeral.

Thanks are very much in order to many people. First to Beverley Slopen, who insisted we go ahead with this despite many arguments to the contrary, all of them mine. There's no reasoning with Beverley Slopen. To Michael Enright, Martin O'Malley, and John Tennyson McLeod, who provided all the good ideas. Special attention is due the Columnists Association of Canada, of which I am privileged to be Recording Secretary. To Rod McQueen, the title specialist, who furnished the title. Peter Taylor took the material and found, if not order in chaos, at least a more perfect disorder. Richard Tallman, the editor, has a fine eye. To *The Toronto Star* – bless her and all who sail in her, particularly Kym Adams who typed much of the manuscript, and Noreen Bramsen, an excellent person in anybody's book. Particular thanks to Hartley Steward, now of the *Toronto Sun*, who invented Slinger and let him roll. Finally to Andrea and Brennan McCabe, for filling up my life, and to my wife, Nora McCabe. She laughs in all the wrong places, but I love her anyway.

Joey Slinger,
the summer solstice, 1985

1

Life, A Beginner's Guide

Staying out of the gutter

Young people are always asking for my advice. My advice to them is always the same: don't end up in the gutter.

Look at what they wear in the gutter. It is not the latest styles. It is unfashionable and filthy, discarded garments out at the knee or elbow, whichever is the relevant joint. The shoes are split and must be stuffed with newspapers to keep out the damp. The laces are frequently broken and knotted and the little plastic things at the tips of the laces have disappeared, that is for certain. Nothing matches.

Look at what they eat in the gutter. It is not wholesome home-cooked meals. It is not junk food. It is trash. Fish innards, canteloupe rinds, tea bags, and a lot of stuff that can no longer be easily classified apart from saying it is green, or very green, or green with orange spots, or mostly orange spots, and so on. That is variety, but variety alone will not sustain a body.

How do people end up in the gutter? The story of each person in the gutter is unique, but they can be broken down into two broad, general themes. (1) Did not tidy up after themselves despite entreaties and, occasionally, threats from parents. Came to express defiance through messiness, later sought solace in it. Finally drifted to the one place in town where they could always be assured of finding a mess. Or (2), are on the lam from heartbreak.

Opportunities for advancement in the gutter are meagre. From time to time some self-debased wretch is hired by a revivalist tent show. Every night he or she comes forward at an appointed moment (usually at a signal from the podium, a hankie dropped, a shrill chord on the steam calliope, a pistol fired, sometimes all three if

15

several wretches are to come forward at once) to relate to the goggle-eyed audience how he or she fell upon wicked ways and ended up in that place whence he or she has so lately been retrieved.

This is not hard work but it is tedious and if there is one thing people in the gutter share it is a despair bred of tedium, so before long they quit and return to the gutter where they can achieve the same despair with less effort and their tedium is not threatened by a stampede from the bleachers as believers rush forward, having been swayed by their tale of degradation.

Is the gutter full of riff-raff? Not necessarily. The percentage of riff-raff in the gutter remains about the same as the percentage in the population at large, slightly lower than in professional groups, slightly higher than in poolrooms, roughly the same as among the idle rich and single parents, and, while the ratio is the same as among academics, there is a great deal less borrowing money and forgetting to pay it back, although since no one in the gutter ever has any money to lend, this latter point may be moot.

In any event, steer clear of the gutter if you're looking for a statement of man's basic nature asserting itself amid the shattered ethos of the once-grand urban experiment, especially if you are inclined to make sweeping generalizations. Which is all by way of saying that your chances of getting stabbed in the back by people in whom you have placed your trust is about the same in the gutter as anywhere else in society, so if you're going to get stabbed in the back, why not do it someplace warm and dry like a plush boardroom on Bay Street or the reading room of an exclusive club?

Avoid gutter language. Gutter language begets gutter thinking begets a gutter lifestyle begets the gutter itself. "Nucular" is an example of gutter language, as in "the impending nucular holocaust." Also the verb "to impact." It is perhaps unfair to say everyone who uses impact as a verb is destined to end up in the gutter, since that includes the entire advertising industry, but there is nothing fair about the gutter. And they may well end up there for other reasons.

Have people in the gutter lost all pride? Definitely. Oh, rarely you'll hear somebody from one gutter say to somebody from another, "My gutter is utterly depraved compared to yours," but usually they forget the subject of the conversation before the sentence is finished.

How to stay out of the gutter: emulate decent members of the community. Listen to their advice. Tidy up after yourself. Avoid heartbreak.

Infighting at the O.V. corral

Dear Slinger,

Just a note to bring you up to date on the gang in the Old Vienna commercial.

It's all off between Sherri and Tod. Sherri started going with Tim who was going with Kerri until she started seeing Tom. Tom and Terri split up an hour ago and now Terri and Tab are an item, or at least they were except Tab seemed to be paying a lot of attention to Gerri when Terri was off chatting with Tod. Gerri had been going steady with Tod until he dumped her for Sherri, and when Gerri started crying on Tom's shoulder it was the last straw for Kerri.

Tom got new penny loafers, which made Tod green with envy because his loafers are a month old. Tod didn't let on to Tom, although he told Kerri that you could always count on Tom to copy everything he did. Tab said that was right – remember when he and Tab and Tim switched from flared jeans to straight-leg cords how Tom switched, too?

Tim came in with his new trophy. It had a little racquetball player on the top. Sherri and Gerri and Kerri all got up and went over to congratulate him, which caused Tom to mention to Tod that if there was one thing he couldn't stand it was a showoff.

While Sherri and Kerri and Gerri went on telling Tim what a wonderful person he was, Terri came and sat with Tab who was feeling blue because the new trophy he came in with an hour before only had a little racquetball racquet on top. While nobody was looking, Tom and Tod went over to their table and took their trophies with the squash players on the tops and put them under their coats and snuck out.

Tim told Tab he wondered what was going through Tom's and Tod's minds that they were still playing such a limp-wristed game as squash. Tab said he figured it was because they didn't have the stuff it takes to play a game that was a real challenge, like racquetball. Tim said they were really out of it.

Kerri decided it was time she re-established her relationship with Terri, so she went and sat with Terri and Tab and said she thought Terri's new shade of lipstick was really sharp. This pleased Terri so much that she asked Kerri where she had found the nail polish she was wearing. Terri said it was the sharpest nail polish she had ever seen and would love to get some.

Since they were being so close, Terri asked Kerri what she thought of Sherri's new pleated skirt and Kerri said that while some people can wear pleats, some people can't. Terri said she knew exactly what she meant. Just then Gerri came over and said she wondered what on earth had been going through Sherri's mind when she bought that pleated skirt.

Then Sherri came over to the table and Kerri and Terri and Gerri told her how much they liked her new skirt. Sherri was really pleased and pulled out her horoscope book. She said her horoscope – she's a Pisces – was she would find happiness and she shouldn't let trials get her down. Gerri, who's a Libra, asked what hers was and Sherri looked it up and said Gerri would find happiness and she shouldn't let trials get her down.

Terri said she'd already looked hers up and for Geminis the word was they would find happiness and they shouldn't let trials get them down. This made Kerri happy because she's a Gemini, too.

Tom and Tod came back in with racquetball trophies and Sherri and Gerri and Terri and Kerri gathered around and congratulated them. Tim told Tab he really didn't have much use for girls who were only interested in guys who won trophies and Tab agreed, but said he wouldn't be surprised if Tom and Tod bought the trophies the same place they'd bought theirs.

Terri came over and sat with them and said she, personally, was mainly interested in a person's feelings. She asked Tab how he was really, deep-down feeling? He said he was feeling fine. Terri said she was glad to hear it. She said she was feeling fine, too.

Tab said it was all off between him and Sherri because Sherri didn't care about feelings. Tim felt like three's company, so he went over to congratulate Tom and Tod on their trophies.

It was a pretty great night. See you.

Luv, Dawn.

Dispensing with women

If Toronto's Cardinal Carter is looking for support for his doctrinal statement that women have no place in the priesthood, he need look no farther than me. I have concluded that women have no place anywhere.

Furthermore, from what I can tell from scientific developments, we will soon be able to dispense with them entirely. This will be a relief.

Until it happens, though, I advise the Cardinal to stay in the priesthood himself. If he were to go into some other line of work and say what he said about there being no place for women in it, he would be yanked into court for violating every human rights statute in the book. That's how powerful women have become. A man can't say what he thinks any more unless he's lucky enough to be barricaded in the *cathedra* and is speaking *ex*.

My position is not reactionary. It doesn't stem, as the church's does, from an ancient effort to stifle competition with a number of middle-eastern religions that were popular at the time of Christ, and which worshipped goddesses, often through the offices of priestesses. Nor is it based on tedious old Samuel Johnson's tedious old dictum, "A woman preaching is like a dog's walking on his hind legs. It is not done well; but you are surprised to find it done at all."

(I was pleased to see the Cardinal say keeping women out of the priesthood is an issue in which there is no room for compromise or middle ground. Until he presented it as such, there had been only one other thoroughly inflexible position in the world. It was discovered by Stephen Jay Gould, the natural historian: "the only truly important and complex debate with no possible stance in between is whether you are for or against the designated hitter rule."

(This means that in every single other aspect of your life, you most likely find yourself in a grey area. No wonder you get confused.)

What got me thinking about how women aren't necessary any more was something a woman wrote. In the introduction to her biography of P.G. Wodehouse, Frances Donaldson said that, "Because of their greater imagination, women do not care for musical-hall jokes, farcical comedy, or any humor that relies on total disregard for the sufferings of innocent characters, while, because of their need to involve themselves, situations of mistaken identity or serious misunderstanding merely arouse their anxiety. They are incapable of isolating the element of humor from all the other aspects of a situation, possibly because traditionally their range of experience has been so circumscribed."

Women have no sense of humour. That's what that means. A sense of humour is a major requirement of the priesthood, because priests like to be able to get off a few killer jokes when they're out with laymen. It shows there's a regular fellow under the surplice. Cardinal

19

Carter himself is no exception. It's also a requirement of just about everything else in life that I can think of.

Things used to work well when women stayed out of the picture. Men could get together for a few laughs and put together a Renaissance or an Industrial Revolution. There would be the occasional war, but the warriors that survived would gather when it was over and laugh about the grand times they had. It was only when they got home to their wives and mothers that they had to put on that what they'd been up to was serious.

Now these wives and mothers are out here in the workplace, in the cockpits of military jets and space shuttles, at the helms of artistic movements. Now everything is deadly serious. And what has it got us? Worldwide inflation. A seventy-two-cent dollar. The threat of a war that no warriors will survive. And Boy George. Now nobody is laughing.

Fortunately, the time of wives and mothers is just about ended. The new phrase is *in vitro*, where children get born in glass beakers in the laboratory, as opposed to *in utero*, the messy, old-fashioned way. Evolution has shown that once there is no more need for a thing, it withers, becomes vestigial – dies off. And science has eliminated the need for women.

One morning, mankind will put on his slippers and shuffle downstairs, expecting to find his breakfast prepared and on the table. The only thing he will find on the table is a note that reads, "I've become extinct. Good-bye."

Bay Streetproofing

The weather is getting nicer and children are spending more time outdoors, so now is the time to Bay Streetproof your child. Children are easy prey for unscrupulous stock promoters and mutual-fund salesmen. These people care nothing for the long-term prosperity of a youngster or the pain a family suffers when a child is forced into bankruptcy through unsound investment practices.

Lately our specially trained analysts at the Bay Streetproofing Institute have seen too many children who have been the victims of cruel mergers. Some don't survive a merger. Some survive, but with their minds and their financial futures severely impaired.

Say Little Johnny (a fictitious child) has spread himself thin through diversification and unprofitable acquisitions. One day he comes out of the variety store having taken a strong position on margin in ju-jubes. A greasy looking character in a trench coat beckons him over to a parked car. What Little Johnny doesn't know is that this greasy looking character is a greenmailer. But how could he know that? Little Johnny is an innocent, trusting child whose parents didn't care enough for his well-being to have him Bay Streetproofed.

The greenmailer covers Little Johnny's margin call on the ju-jubes and begins to acquire shares in his other holdings – paying more than the going market price – until he comes close to owning controlling interest in Johnny's whole family. To stave this off, the parents must find a "white knight," a sympathetic corporation that will buy out the greenmailer and leave the current management in place.

A white knight might be Nabisco, it might be Standard Oil of New Jersey, and even though it might successfully prevent the takeover, the fact remains that Little Johnny's market value has been wildly inflated and his once happy family will never again know the solace and comfort of their private concerns, not since they have become a wholly owned subsidiary.

Had Little Johnny been Bay Streetproofed he would have avoided buying on margin when he didn't have enough savings to cover the cost, he would have taken care to check the price-against-earnings ratio before acquiring stocks when he was already overdiversified, and he would have avoided talking to the greasy character in the trench coat outside the variety store.

But don't fall into the trap of thinking the only danger to an unwary child is from the stereotyped creepy dealer who lurks around playgrounds and other kiddies' hangouts. Often they are quite normal-looking citizens, even neighbours. Take the case of Little Millicent. (Another fictitious child, but don't fall into the trap of thinking only fictitious children run afoul of sleazy promoters. Bay Streetproof your child whether it is fictitious or not.)

One warm afternoon Little Millicent was playing with her dolls in her backyard when her neighbour, a jolly old gentleman she had known all her young life, invited her to come over into his yard where she could play in his sprinkler and have something cool to drink.

Not thinking twice, because she had never been Bay Streetproofed, Little Millicent blithely accepted the invitation. Neither Little Millicent nor her unsuspecting parents realized that their jolly old neighbour was, in fact, a commodities broker. When the shaken child was finally restored to her family, she had purchased more than $500,000 worth of contracts for the future delivery of pork bellies, cocoa, and soybeans. The shame was more than she could endure. Little Millicent's parents had to liquidate all their holdings, including the family home, to meet commitments a Bay Streetproofed child never would have made.

Even Registered Retirement Savings Plans, especially if self-directed, can blow up in the face of a child who hasn't been Bay Streetproofed. The temptation to load an RRSP with high-performance mutual funds can be great, and often the highest-flying funds were started by people who are currently felons or are living beyond the law in such pestilential hell holes as Nicaragua. Once started down the market's slippery slope your child could end up the same. Don't let it happen. Bay Streetproof. A child's securities are a nation's security.

Advice to the lifelorn

This is an advice column.

– Stand up straight. Posture is probably the most important human quality. People, when they stand all gibbled-up, don't get enough blood to their brains and they can come to some pretty strange conclusions. This does not necessarily mean they are stupid, just stooped. People with good posture go a lot farther in life than slouchers. Look at Queen Elizabeth. She is actually 6-foot-1 but has such terrible posture she only looks 5-foot-3. At that, she still got to be queen. Think how much farther she might have gone if she had stood up straight!

– Be born into a wealthy family. There is little question that wealthy people do better in the long run than poor people. And people born wealthy don't have to waste so much time accumulating wealth as people who are not born wealthy and decide to become so. If it is too late for you to be born into a wealthy family the next best thing is to find a wealthy family and hang around with them. Show up for meals. Stand outside the bathroom in the morning holding your toothbrush and waiting your turn. Wealthy people have little interest in details. Before long they will conclude you are one of theirs and buy you a pony!

– Shorten up on the bat. If you are having trouble getting around on the ball, you can increase bat-speed by choking up on the bat. A shorter grip will also help you to pull the ball.

– Accentuate the positive! Eliminate the negative!

– Use gift-wrap instead of shelf-paper to line your drawers. Assuredly shelf-paper has come a long way in the last few years and can be purchased in a number of attractive colours and patterns but it still carries about it a drab, utilitarian aura. By using festive gift-wrap as a drawer-liner you can give yourself a little lift on those grey days! Imagine opening your sock drawer to discover that you have reached the end of the clean socks. Gloom! But, if the drawer is lined with colourful paper that says, "Compliments of the season!" or is covered with bunny rabbits holding banners that say "A birthday surprise!" you will feel cheered up and appreciate that life can be worthwhile!

– Take up scat-singing. It is the ideal conversation starter and a good way to relieve tension during difficult negotiations. Say you meet Henry Kissinger at the bus stop and can't think of a thing to say. If you can sing scat, you only have to go, "Hey, skeeby-skeeby whado, bow row fee-deedly-oh," and the ice will be broken! Shuttle diplomats swear by it!

– Run to daylight!

– Move the part in your hair. If you want to break out of a rut, moving the part in your hair can provide good psychological leverage. Move if from left to right or right to left. Or, if you want a big change, move it down to your knee or even further afield. If you are bald you can accomplish the same thing by using felt pens to brighten your scalp with interesting designs!

– When sending threatening letters, don't send a pasted-up note made of words cut from comic books or the *National Enquirer*. People will think you are low class. Use words cut from academic journals or, if rushed, *Time* magazine!

– To thine own self be true!

– Show him who's the real boss. The next time Hopeless Harry comes home drunk for dinner and brings his boss with him without any advance warning, serve macaroni and cheese. He'll soon get the message!

– To thine own self be true in thine own fashion!

– Make your own compost. Starting a compost heap is a lot more fun than most people think. And with fall coming this is the perfect time to start one. You don't even need a garden! A lot of apartment dwellers look enviously at people with backyards, wishing they, too, could derive the pleasure of making their own compost. Well, they can! A dark closet is ideal, or the bathtub. Soon you will have more compost than you ever dreamed possible!

Quiet on the breakfast front

As generalizations go, one of the safest is that people who talk during breakfast have serious emotional disorders. And people who talk before breakfast are perverts.

By talk I mean chat, chatter, converse, carry on a conversation, ask how you're feeling. Tell you how they're feeling. Babble. About anything. Some communication is necessary, no doubt. Pass the sugar. Where's the stupid jelly? A basic civility ought to be maintained.

If the house is on fire, one's fellow occupants should be informed. Getting up from the table and going outside without a word, leaving everyone else to be incinerated simply because you despise morning conversation, is extreme behaviour.

Businessmen, and, more lately, politicians, have taken to holding breakfast meetings. That explains why the nation's industrial strategy is as lively as a poached egg and looks sour around the mouth. There should be a ninety-day cooling-off period, actually more like a warming-up period, on all decisions taken before ten in the morning. The ice doesn't go out in our brains until after ten in the morning. It is still winter up there at breakfast-time.

Politicians and businessmen hold these early morning meetings because, they say, they want to get a good jump on the day. It is a waste of time. No matter how good a jump you get on the day, sooner or later it catches up and comes crashing down around you. The only way to approach the day is from ambush. Keep quiet. Let it think you're paying no attention at all. It will get on with its chores. The minute its back is turned, sneak over and cold-cock it with the coffee percolator. That will keep it out of your way.

Breakfasts in my childhood were blissful. My father and mother and brother and I didn't just not talk to one another in the morning, we didn't like one another in the morning. The way four people, operating independently and in total silence, washed, dressed, ate, and got themselves on their ways is a model of détente the nations of the world would do well to emulate.

We saved familial intercourse for the supper table, when the blood

24

was up and we could fight at top volume. That's when I began to work on a technique that has served me well in social situations ever since, one I came to perfect: leaving the table in tears. I don't believe there is a more effective method of showing just how wronged you have been, or how misunderstood you are, or of injecting a good jolt of guilt into the people around you, than leaving the table in tears. I recommend it.

But in the morning, any display of emotion, apart from veiled loathing – veiled is essential – is inappropriate. Especially later in life, when hangovers become crueller and more frequent, and when an unpleasant physiological change occurs that makes it impossible to sleep in. What it is about the body that wants you to be awake to share its pain is beyond me.

In fact, the whole business of pain is beyond me. Biologists and the like rave on about what a wondrous organism the body is. For example, it developed pain as an alarm system, to alert us that something is awry, that we have done something that is bad for us and we should stop. That strikes me as a crock. If the body is as great as it's cracked up to be, why did it develop such a crude alarm system? One that hurts? Why didn't it develop instead a little bell that rings? Ring, ring. Oops, burned my finger. Ring, ring. Oops, gall bladder's acting up. Ring, ring. Oops, had a little too much to drink last night. *That* would be wondrous.

If a bell ringing before ten in the morning is unduly stressful, you could replace it with soft chimes.

As for lovers talking up a storm in the morning, this is revolting. Between the sun's going down and the sun's coming up, as it were, nothing much has happened to you that you both don't know about already. So why rehash it? If an apology is called for, do it in writing. The sound of All-Bran turning soggy is as much noise as any sensible person can stand at breakfast.

Marital arts

Not long ago the chief justice of the Ontario Supreme Court's trial division said couples planning to marry should be required to take a course in how best to make their union work. He thought this would reduce the number of divorces and the high costs.

Being a person who got married on a whim and a shoestring and then paid an enormous price mentally and financially to get out of it, I agree with the judge wholeheartedly. In fact, I have been giving careful thought to things he would probably want included in the curriculum of a premarital course, such as:

– Become A Financial Genius. It is widely recognized that most marital stress arises over financial disagreements. There can be little to disagree about, however, if the marriage unit becomes what is known as filthy rich. Therefore, any mate who wants to ensure a lasting marriage must become filthy rich.

– Have Perfect Sex. After finances, the greatest source of discord between mates is sex. This is easily resolved if the partners have only perfect sex. This is generally defined as an orgasm whenever and as often as either mate wishes, to be followed by an ice cream sundae or a good cry, as preferred.

– Raise Perfect Children. Too often a marriage on the skids can be traced to children who caused dissension between mates. A spoiled and demanding child can try any parent's patience; a child having difficulties at school can sow doubt in mates' minds and make them feel helpless; a child who begins to deal smack or runs with a motorcycle gang that destroys your house during an orgy of beer and amphetamines can mean tribulation in the strongest heart and cause mates to blame one another for having failed. To avoid this, have nothing but children who are beautifully behaved, who always say please and thank you, who attend Upper Canada College and win scholarships, and who become doctors and marry Eatons.

– Avoid Argument. Nothing puts a bigger crimp in a marriage than arguing. Arguments can lead to anything from mates not speaking to one another to mates planting axes in one another's foreheads. Mates must never mount the high horse of principle. When one mate says something that is completely far-fetched or half-cocked or just plain booga-booga, the other mate must say, "Why darling, now you put it that way, I see your point and agree with you completely," or "Right as usual, honey."

– Keep An Open Mind. Too often marriages founder because one mate has a closed mind. Say one mate doesn't make it home one night and phones the next day and, in a slurred voice, says he or she was carried off by large vegetables from Alpha Centauri. Or say one mate says the car rose into the air as if by magic, while he or she stood helplessly by, and whanged into a tree and got all bent. And say the mate who gets told these stories had already formed a preconceived notion and had become inflexible. Then a wedge would be driven into the marriage bond that dynamite couldn't dislodge. To preserve the marriage, a mate must keep an open mind and merely say, "Oh, my goodness. Oh, my goodness," and wring his or her hands.

– Mate Recognition. It is important that you be able to recognize your mate. Nothing is more depressing than to awaken after fifteen years of marriage and roll over and look at your mate and have to say, "Excuse me, but who are you?" And then, on being informed of the identity, to have to say, "I'm afraid there's been a terrible mistake."

It is vital to note one or two distinguishing characteristics (a mole, a scar, an obsession with spreading peanut butter on the windows while railing against Presbyterians) and to write them along with his or her name on a piece of paper and keep it in your wallet.

This will save time and embarrassment if some day, perhaps after leaving a party or a bar, you find yourself about to pile into the sack with someone you don't recall having bumped into around the family home. You quickly pull out your Mate-I.D. checklist and if nothing matches you say, "I'm sorry, but it would be wrong." And you go straight home, your marriage saved.

That should do it. It's reassuring that someone in so lofty a position as a chief justice should have had such a down-to-earth idea.

Bogging down in tofu

There was a bumper sticker on a van ahead of me at the stoplight. "Have you rinsed your tofu today?" it read. Something came over me when I saw it that left me unable to proceed when the light changed.

The van pulled away. Drivers behind me honked, then wheeled out and gunned past, yelling insults. As light after light changed and streams of cars honked and snarled by me, I sat there, stuck, not in traffic, but in a jam of despond.

It had come to me, in that moment, that I was a thorough-going phony.

Listen, I didn't know whether that line on the bumper sticker was a joke. And I didn't know whether it was a joke because I didn't know what tofu was. I didn't know whether it was little green things like sprouts or little brown things like raisins or jiggly and yucky like bean curd or something runny that you spread.

Yet, I mourned, this had never stopped me from using the word. Not just using it, but using it in a disparaging way, with scorn in my voice, when I described people who flitted after whatever will-o'-the-wisp of style happened to be in.

Tofu implied bland and superficial and holier-than-thou in matters of taste the way "ten-speed-liberal" used to imply those things in matters of politics. I would say, "They probably eat a lot of tofu," and drip condescension, as only a red-meat eater can drip it.

Now I realized I didn't have a clue what I was talking about. My whole being, my sense of individuality, had been based on feeling superior to the superficial tofu eaters of the world. Now I saw that I was more superficial than they.

It was an existential moment, stalled there on a busy city street, the object of hostility and obscenities as strangers tried to manoeuvre around me in the noon traffic. And my despair doubled, tripled, because when I realized it was an existential moment, I also realized I didn't know what existential meant.

I have used the word for years. Hardly a conversation went by that I didn't fling it in. I thought it lent a deep and brooding quality to what otherwise would be ordinary gossip. "But for an existential flaw in her psyche she would have returned my phone calls." That sort of thing.

When I thought about it honestly, though, existentialism was just so much tofu to me, a meaningless word I used in the hope of lending gravity to ideas as substantial as dustballs.

The traffic had begun to snarl in front of me as impatient drivers tried to cut in and blocked oncoming vehicles. Nothing could get into or out of the cross-streets. The entire economy was coming to a halt around me.

As I watched it my despair grew into hopelessness, because I had no idea what the economy was. Once the economy had been Keynesian. I would rise in the morning and look out on a Keynesian economy. When something happened I would shrug it off. "Keynesian influences," I would say, although I didn't know from doodly-squat what a Keynesian influence was.

Then the economy became post-Keynesian, then neo-post-Keynesian. But when I looked out I saw the same things I had always seen. I couldn't tell the difference. And yet this ignorance didn't stop me from continuing to be a part of the economy, from suffering the effects of inflation, from showing up in statistics.

Sitting there in the clotting traffic, while drivers got out of their cars and slammed their doors and shook their fists at me, I realized I could no longer relate to the economy.

I couldn't even relate to relationships. "This isn't a relationship," someone always said, her lip trembling. "This is just two people being together." I had thought that's what a relationship was. Only a real phony would think a thing like that.

I couldn't stand sitting in the same car as such a phony. I got out and was walking away when a policeman who had made his way through the stalled cars and the enraged mob of drivers said, "What seems to be the trouble, buddy?"

"Tofu," I said.

"I know how you feel," he said.

Bathroom humours

There are only two things that drag me from my bed these nights. One is the call of Nature. The other is the call of the Muse. In my business it is sometimes difficult to tell which is which.

Toward three the other a.m. I found myself in my nightgown hunched over the table writing in my notebook, "CBC vs. toilet paper." I'm at a loss to say which category that fits into.

I do know that if an idea comes along during the night and I don't write it down, it will be gone in the morning and have left no forwarding address.

As Alice records in *Through The Looking Glass*: "The horror of that moment," the King went on, "I shall never, *never* forget!"

"You will, though," the Queen said, "if you don't make a memorandum of it."

When morning came the memorandum in my notebook seemed powerfully cryptic, but I fished with it for a while and finally reeled in that I had once been privy to (this isn't going to be easy, is it?) a confidential CBC memorandum that had to do with how toilet paper was to be dealt with in television commercials since, to protect the delicate, the broadcasters had decided neither the words "toilet" nor "paper" could be mentioned. The bards of euphemy decreed that to prevent the entire nation's being laid out with the vapours, the only fit phrase was "bathroom tissue."

Why it should have occurred to me in my tortured half-slumber that this might be worth writing about I have no idea. But since we've come this far, we might as well give it a whirl. Leave us not be squeamish.

– Among all the things I don't understand in this life, the thing I don't understand most is scented toilet paper.

– People who fold the corners of the end toilet paper sheet under to form a tidy V when company is coming have problems so extreme that they should immediately seek professional counselling.

– My first wife was an early Whole-Earther. To combat pollution, she refused to purchase coloured toilet paper, maintaining that the dyes contaminated the world's water supply when it was disposed of. When she left me, I went and bought a roll of toilet paper that was not only coloured, but was decorated with a floral pattern. I used nothing else for years. Viewed from the proper perspective, it made me feel better about a whole lot of things.

– Of all economy measures, the most annoying are the elliptical toilet-paper rollers in some public washrooms that go wobble-wobble and permit you to pull off one, or at most two sheets at a time. They are devices of the devil and bring out the vandal in me.

– My friend Daniel was thought, by his mother, to be slow to grasp what is referred to as "toilet training." Concerned, his mother consulted a pediatrician who told her not to worry. "How many people do you know your age," he asked, "who aren't toilet trained?"

– My friend Anthony eagerly accepted the concept of toilet training but found the details and the timing were sometimes more than he could manage. This concerned his father, since Anthony was beginning nursery school and there was considerable danger he might have what is referred to as "an accident." "Don't worry," the teacher told Anthony's father. "At ten o'clock we have toilet."

– My first day of kindergarten I was sent home because I had an accident.

– When someone goes into the bathroom and closes the door and continues to talk to me, I don't listen. I ignore them completely.

– I have been led to understand that, in general, women don't read on the toilet. If this is true, it is a shameful waste of time and explains why women can't keep intellectual pace with men. Piled on the back of my toilet are *The Complete Works of William Shakespeare*, *Remembrances of Things Past* (4 vols.) by Marcel Proust, *Finnegan's Wake* by James Joyce, the take-out and delivery menu from Crow's Nest Pizza, Hansard since 1958, a July, 1981, copy of *Sports Illus-*

trated, the report of the Kent Royal Commission inquiry into corporate concentration in the ownership of newspapers, and *Swamp Vixen* by Orrie Hitt.

I don't worry that Nature calls during the night far more often than the Muse. It gives me a chance to improve my mind.

Getting mugged

Since it is a guiding principle of the society in which we live that we are innocent until proven guilty, the inclusion of our photographs on our drivers' licences must not mean that the province of Ontario and the agents who enforce its traffic laws – the police – believe we might be guilty of lying when we present a licence to them and claim it is our own. There is no need to prove we are telling the truth. They take it for granted that we are. Therefore there must be some other reason they want to put our pictures on our licences. What might it be?

1. There are days, and these days seem to come more frequently, when a person wakes up and asks, Who am I? Where am I going? What is the meaning of Life? Where did the wheels come off? What does any of this matter? And so on. And so forth. These questions provoke feelings of insecurity, of inadequacy, and frequently lead to bouts of depression requiring treatment by qualified head-shrinkers.

Head-shrinkers rarely accept the province's medical fee schedule, insisting on extra payment. But now, a soul lost to himself in despair can look in the mirror and pull out his driver's licence and discover then and there who he is. The answers to the other questions will automatically fall into place. The savings in head-shrinking bills will be enormous.

2. While the police and government are bound by principle to believe us when we tell them who we are, there are some people who have no principles and are not so bound. My mother, for instance. My mother says, "You're no son of mine. No son of mine would live the way you live. No son of mine would dress the way you dress. A son of mine would have a real job and not waste his life in foolery. And no son of mine would be as old as you are."

Or my boss. When somebody complains about something I've done my boss denies that I work for him. "A firm with a reputation such as ours wouldn't have a what-not such as him working for us. We wouldn't let him in the door. Nosireebob."

With my picture on my licence I'd have them over a barrel.

3. It will come in especially handy every time you have to go down and pick up lottery winnings. Before handing over your million the lottery scrutineers can check to see that the picture on the licence looks like the person holding the ticket.

No – wait! – they don't have any record of who bought the ticket in the first place. So it would make no difference if an unscrupulous person has steamed the genuine picture off the licence and substituted his own. Even if we were all fingerprinted it wouldn't help. The only solution to this persistent problem is for the government to hire agents to follow us everywhere and report on our doings.

4. Some days we think nothing can go wrong. All is right with the world. We get the euphoric feeling that life is good and will go on forever. Well, it won't. Let's not kid ourselves. One of these days, bingo, and that was all she wrote.

To help us remember that and avoid making appointments we won't be able to keep, the government is putting our pictures on our licences. Then we can carry in our wallets an accurate measure of how much and how rapidly we're aging.

When we meet old friends we haven't seen in twenty years and they say, "Why, you don't look a day older," we can whip out our licences and show them just how wrong they are.

5. The government worries that we will forget it. When we get our licences now it happens so efficiently – they just show up in the mail – we don't even think about it. Too much of this and we would soon forget that the government is working constantly on our behalf. But we'll remember it if the government complicates our lives at every turn. By requiring a picture they have figured out how to make difficult something that was becoming entirely too easy.

6. I don't know about you, but I am constantly mistaken for Robert Redford. If you are, too, you'll know that it isn't exactly fun. People always insisting on buying you drinks in bars. Strange women following you home and making unusual suggestions. With a picture on my licence I will be able to show them it is a case of mistaken identity. Then we can have a good laugh and forget the whole thing.

Daycare for ducks

Ripley, in his Believe It or Not! the other day, said "the female silvery-cheeked hornbill seals herself in a hollow tree trunk until her chicks are grown. The family is fed by the male 10 to 20 times a day through a chink in the bark!"

Way to go, Ripley! I cried sadly. How to perpetuate the old male-female stereotypes! The moss-backed old anti-feminists will have a field day when they get ahold of this!

The moss-backed old anti-feminists – MOAFs – believe there is a natural way of doing things and that Nature decreed Mammy should stay shut up at home tending the chicklets while Pappy goes out into the big world and rustles up the bacon (or, in the case of the silvery-cheeked hornbill, the small poisonous creatures) and brings it home to his brood, as is considered his manly duty.

If the female ups and dabbles in the workplace and sticks the kids in daycare, the natural order will be cast into ruction and civilization will careen into Hell in a basket labelled "Equal Pay for Work of Equal Value." "It just ain't right," the MOAFs say, and Ripley's dragging out the silvery-cheeked hornbill will harden them in their narrow, reactionary ways.

Ripley very conveniently neglected to mention that the wall the hornbill seals herself into the tree behind is a wall she builds out of her own droppings! Which are viscid at first but harden on exposure to air! And in order to carry out her business, she defecates at high velocity through the narrow entrance slit! If the MOAFs think *that* provides a wholesome environment for nurturing unformed minds, one gags at the thought of what one might see behind the lace curtains of their rose-covered cottages. The Children's Aid has its work cut out.

What the MOAFs don't know, relying as they do on Ripley for news of cultural consequence, is that there are some pretty liberated birds flapping around out there, birds that don't care to fortify themselves behind the crumbling conventions of Victorian mores.

Take the red-breasted merganser, a duck with a long saw-toothed bill. (Male red-breasted mergansers have been heard to exclaim "Yeow!" just before making love, an ambiguous exclamation if ever there was one.)

The female lays eight or ten eggs and, after hatching, the ducklings trail along on her apron strings for a month or longer. How sweet and motherly she seems – until you stop one day to tally up the tots splashing in her wake and count twenty or more junior mergansers. Hey. What gives?

What gives is duck daycare. Since Poppa departs early on in the proceedings, female mergansers find they are single mothers and have to go out and get jobs, mainly fishing. They park the kids with some obliging female, put their faces on, and go to work. This gives the MOAFs palpitations, but studies show that almost all these young mergansers, although deprived of the loving attention of their own true mothers, grow into responsible ducks.

Figures are hard to come by, but it is safe to say that few mergansers end up with their names on the police blotter or otherwise become burdens on society.

If you think that's enlightened, get a load of the phalarope, a streamlined little number, sort of like the sandpiper except it has this thing about swimming around and around in circles.

The phalaropes have gone in for role-reversal. The females are all flash in the Saturday-night stepping-out duds more usually found on the males of a species. The guys are drab, drab, drab. The female takes charge of romancing and beats up on any other lady who throws a wink her sweetie's way.

She does lay the eggs – *some* things are written in stone – but get this: as soon as she does she plops the old man on them and takes off! She's a gone bird! Wings away to the bright lights, never to be heard from by Dad and the kids again. She has better things to do than be tied down by all this boring family bunk.

What this means is that almost anything you do is something that comes naturally somewhere or other. If the MOAFs want to believe Ripley or not, it doesn't matter. He's not telling the whole story.

Some day I'll tell you about the brown-headed cowbird. After the brown-headed cowbird comes the revolution.

Swing-trees

There are three swing-trees that I have found – there are probably more; they tend to be out of the way, hard to get to, and not immediately noticeable unless they are being swung on – along the Don River and its tributary creeks.

Swing-trees are trees from which ropes are suspended, usually high up to give the swinger a better arc. The swinger climbs up on something, a tree branch or higher up the bank, takes a firm grip on the rope, gives a mighty backward push with the legs for momentum and then, allez-oop, swings out and up in the sky so high, lets go the rope and plummets, ploosh! into the water.

The idea of putting so much as a toe in Toronto's Don River might give a lot of us the willies, but swing-tree swingers are not notably fastidious. They are in it for the sweeping thrill of the swing, for the giddy weightlessness that overtakes them at the far end of the arc, and for the free, tummy-flipping fall.

Some tree-swingers will claim they are in it for the sharp, refreshing plunge into a cool swimming hole, but true tree-swingers will recognize them for dilettantes.

One of the swing-trees is north of Sheppard Avenue, in the elbow of a little creek that winds southward under the intersection of Bayview and Finch. It involves quite a bit of construction. Boards have been nailed to trees to form ladders, handholds, and platforms. It is the sort of conspicuous display of planning one might expect in a nook of such an upwardly mobile neighbourhood, where even hacking around calls for architects and elaborate expenditures of materials and effort. It is a project.

The other two are along stretches of the river much nearer the inner city and are conspicuous, if anything, for primitive simplicity. One is conspicuous right now for not even having its rope hung on this, the second day of July, prime swinging time.

But then, a lackadaisical approach to everything, especially tree-swinging, is the mark of a true tree-swinger.

The ropeless swing-tree is just south of the Pottery Road bridge, right beside a tiny, secret, perfect beach and the rope, when it's hung, hangs from a fork in a willow several storeys up, well out over the water. No little recklessness is required to tie it up there. But then, recklessness comes as naturally as riding a bus to a true tree-swinger.

The third, and the best by my measure, is on the edge of thick woods under the high bank that Thorncliffe Park commands. How lovely and adventurous it must feel to wind down through the trees from the hot, high-rise-studded plain to the cool river edge and, hidden from the gaze of the thousands confined in their stacking boxes, swing madly out and up to float for an instant in mid-air.

Rope-swinging was formative in my development; two ropes in particular stand out. One hung from a druidical elm in my backyard and the other from a high beam in a barn near Parry Sound.

Neither offered water landings. The one at home started as an ordinary swing, but order gave way to disorder. The seat was ditched, the ropes were twisted together, a saw horse became a launching pad, and the serious business of swinging through childish fantasies, out and up to tumble in a heap on the grass, began.

The rope in the barn was challenging, hanging as it did far over the drive floor, the gaping chasm between the crossbeams where you departed and the raised hay mow a perilous distance across the way where, you certainly hoped, you arrived in a puff of ages-old hay. Nerve was called for. There were always higher beams to swing from, and here the first, scant inklings of wisdom started to revolve in the mind. It's interesting how what once was the shame of chickening out gets translated into the pride of common sense.

Common sense, though, once it gains the least hold on a person, soon has him locked in a full nelson and, soon enough after that, has him trussed up in what very much resembles a straitjacket.

But that is something the true tree-swinger knows deep down inside. Every swing, after all, ends with the swinger suddenly coming down to earth, or into the muddy Don.

That is why true tree-swingers swing as long as they can and never, years and years later, ever really admit they have stopped.

2
Talking Turkey

Dog-geared

Everybody who acquires a dog says one thing they're going to do for sure is teach the dog to drive. It's important, especially in the city, they say. They say it sure would come in handy.

Invariably they end up not doing it. Here are some of the reasons they give: "Too busy." "Forgot." "Dog got too old." "Short dog, can't see over dashboard." "No car."

What they're really saying is that they didn't have the patience to teach their pet how to operate a motor vehicle or confidence in their ability to instil in the animal not just an appreciation of the rules of the road, but respect for the safety of others.

There is nothing quite as dangerous as a poorly trained dog at the wheel of an automobile. The potential for serious damage to other motorists as well as to pedestrians and to property cannot be overstated and is plainly reflected in the cost of insuring a canine driver.

But there is no escaping the fact that the owner of a dog that causes an accident while at the wheel is as much to blame as the dog for having failed to prepare it properly. It does no good merely to teach the dog the basics and hope it will pick up the rest as it speeds along.

But neither can you measure the pride an owner will feel in helping his pet become a true master of the highway.

Teach by example. Dogs have what amounts to a sixth sense, an uncanny ability to sense their masters' feelings, and if you are lackadaisical about wearing your seatbelt or checking the rearview mirror before pulling out to overtake another vehicle, the dog will be lackadaisical, too.

Be firm. Give commands in an authoritative voice. If you say, "Stop the car, nice doggie," in a sing-song, cooing tone, don't be surprised if the dog thinks you are simply chit-chatting and proceeds at a high rate of speed through a crosswalk full of pedestrians who will be forced to scramble for their lives.

It is imperative that your dog understands that driving lessons are not playtime. Whatever you do, don't laugh at your dog's efforts. You might find it terribly funny if the dog forgets to put the car in reverse while parallel parking and smashes into the car in front, but it is a mistake to let on. Most dogs are desperately eager to please their masters and if you laugh when that happens, the dog will continue to do it under the impression that collisions make you happy.

The first step is to accustom your dog to using the steering wheel, which is by no means instinctive or natural behaviour. Don't try to teach it to steer with its paws. Dogs lack adequate fingers for grasping a steering wheel, and efforts to compensate for this by tying the dog's paws to the wheel or by tying twigs to the dog's paws to approximate fingers are needlessly cruel.

It is a dog's inclination to pick up objects in its mouth and it is far and away easiest and safest to teach it to hold the wheel the same way. Teach this with a system of quasi-rewards: smear the wheel with raw beef as an inducement and always carry some raw beef with you to re-apply in case the dog licks the wheel clean, something that can happen during a long trip, and decides to curl up and go to sleep. A cheap cut of beef should be satisfactory.

Remember that dogs can't read. While it is fortunate that many traffic signs and stop lights come in readily identifiable shapes and colours, written words are meaningless and you shouldn't expect your dog to find a specific exit from a freeway or understand detour and construction signs. When you let your dog drive off in the car by itself, make sure it travels by a familiar route.

Another thing to remember is that your dog is not human, no matter how much it seems to understand what you tell it to do, or how adept it becomes behind the wheel. It remains, at bottom, a dog with all a dog's natural instincts.

If a squirrel or a cat dashes across the road in front of the car, it is in the dog's nature to give chase and you must be prepared for the occasional wild ride down laneways and through backyards.

At first you will be embarrassed to come to a crashing halt against a tree in a stranger's garden while your driver barks furiously at some terrified creature in the branches. Before too long you'll get used to it.

Gone LEGO

"This is the last time I'm going to call you," she yelled from downstairs. "Put away your LEGO and get down here for dinner."

I paid no attention. I was concentrating on the problem of getting my little LEGO knights from their LEGO castle beside my dresser up into space so they could shop at the LEGO space-platform supermarket I had just constructed that was orbiting my bed.

The most practical solution was to put LEGO rocketpacks on the little LEGO horses the knights rode. It worked perfectly. Up they flew.

"If you don't get down here this minute, I will break your dog," she yelled.

Now it was urgent to build attachments on the LEGO spacemen's omniceptors so each could carry a knight to fight the Vorgons if the Vorgons attacked the supermarket, which they all of a sudden did.

There was a pitched battle. Bits of LEGO flew around the bedroom. Vorgons went spiralling away in flames, crumbled piles of shot-up omniceptors and horses filled the space supermarket's aisles. There was a shattering crash.

"There," she yelled. "I broke your dog. That'll teach you to come when dinner's ready."

I raced downstairs. In a thousand pieces on the kitchen floor were the remains of my dog. It had taken days to build that dog out of LEGO. It was a big dog, bigger than a German shepherd. "Just when the Vorgons launch a surprise attack, you break my dog! What a wretched thing to do," I said.

"I hated that stupid dog," she said. "When you started walking it around the block, the neighbours realized you were a lunatic. I was ashamed to go outside."

Sorrowfully I gathered up the pieces. "Other men your age," she said, "they drink too much, or they gamble, or they take up with a popsy from the office. But not you. You couldn't do something rational like that. You have to play with LEGO."

"LEGO is not play," I said, sweeping the last of my dog into a bag. "LEGO is life." I went up to my room, closed the door, and lay sadly on my LEGO bed. I looked at the books I had made out of LEGO that lined my LEGO shelves, at my LEGO clothes in the closet, at the orbiting supermarket from which columns of LEGO smoke still rose, the aftermath of the Vorgon attack.

For comfort I put a LEGO block in my mouth and I must have dozed off and swallowed it because when I wakened it was with a pervading sense of plasticness and a realization that I now possessed superhuman powers. LEGO powers. I had become LEGOMAN.

And LEGOMAN knew that, somewhere, a child was starving. I sped off in my LEGO all-terrain vanicopter with its sky-spy radar antenna and found the starving child weeping in misery. I pulled out my LEGO relief rescue kit and whipped up a burger and presented it to the child. "You'll be all right now, little pardner," I said.

"Are you crazy?" said the child. "This burger is made out of LEGO."

"LEGO is the answer to the world's needs," I said. "Durable and very tasty." He began to sob piteously and I was about to build him some LEGO French fries when my LEGO sense began to tingle and I knew that, somewhere, there was a prime minister in need of fiscal policy.

I jumped into my laser-powered LEGO limousine and in moments found the prime minister struggling with the economy. "LEGOMAN at your service," I said, pulling out my LEGO recovery kit and putting together a fiscal policy. "There you are, big fellow," I said.

"But this is just a whole bunch of LEGO stuck together every which way," he said. I explained that it was better than anything else he had and, more important, it preserved the principle of universality since nothing was more universal than LEGO. He was about to protest when my LEGO sense told me Vorgons were attacking my bedroom again.

In a flash I was there, fending them off with all the LEGO resources at my command, when my wife walked in. She looked around at the carnage littering the floor and said, "This has got to stop."

And you know, she was right. So I took her apart and put her back in the LEGO box. In the morning I will build a new wife, one that isn't so cranky. Right now I have my hands full with the Vorgons.

My reign as Miss Canada

What with the pageant coming up, I've been thinking about Miss Canada. I've been thinking how it would be if my mother hadn't kept me in dresses. One time mothers used to put baby boys in kind of like dresses. My mother kept me in them. If you know my mother, you'll know stranger things have happened. And that's how I ended up getting chosen Miss Canada.

My brother, he worked hard at school and now he's a doctor. But me, I was always too busy entering pageants to apply myself to my studies. First I got to be Miss Teen Guelph, then, the next year, Miss County of Wellington. My father said, "That's all very well, but a man can't spend his whole life being a beauty queen. Look at your brother. He's a doctor."

But I guess I had stars in my eyes. And it wasn't exactly the hardest work on earth. All you had to do was get your makeup on straight, stand around in a swimsuit, and give an impromptu speech on "What Canada Means To Me." Next thing you know you're Miss Ontario and packing your bags to go off to the Miss Canada Pageant, which is on national TV.

The thing about the Miss Canada Pageant is there's a talent segment. Most of the girls do one of the standards, play the guitar or tap-dance or lip-synch to a recording by the Pointer Sisters. What I did was clean a fish. That's what cinched it for me, I think, because the judges looked a little sceptical about a contestant with hairy legs who walked over on his ankles in his high heels.

Some of the other contestants looked pretty queasy when I hauled out my jack-knife and a pickerel and started to hack into it. One of the girls even threw up. She ended up being named Miss Congeniality, which tells you something about the calibre of beauty contest judging, even at the Miss Canada level, but I'm not complaining.

We reached the moment when, you know, the tension was unbearable and it was third runnerup, second runnerup, first runnerup, and then, me. Well, a good many of the girls started to cry, tears being customary in these circumstances, but me, I didn't. I was, as they said next day in the paper, dry-eyed. I mean, look, all my buddies back home, they thought it was kind of peculiar that I wore dresses. After football practice we'd go back to the gym and shower and change and they'd put on their jeans and runners and I'd put on my dress and pantyhose and flats.

They put up with that. But now, what if they saw me on national TV and I burst into tears? They'd think I was a suck.

So they stuck the crown on me and the robe and I grabbed the roses and hobbled down the runway on my ankles – I don't believe

I'll ever get the hang of heels – and when the cameras were on me I thought how impressed all my buddies would be and I just gave them the old thumbs up.

My mother said it was the happiest moment of her life. I don't know about my father – we haven't spoken for some time.

The next morning I was interviewed on *Canada A.M.* The interviewer said it was the first time she had ever interviewed a Miss Canada with a beard.

I said I expected that was the case. Then I offered to clean a fish for her, but she said they had to take a break for a commercial.

Miss Canada usually has a busy year during her reign, what with fashion shows and endorsements and supermarket openings. I went to them at first, but the only people who'd show up were picketers from church groups with placards saying children shouldn't be allowed to see such a thing and eventually the sponsors asked if I wouldn't mind just staying at home.

And my social life picked up for a while. There are a lot of guys who want to date a Miss Canada. But the thrill would seem to wear off fairly early on in the evening when they'd excuse themselves to go to the washroom and never come back. That's something you probably don't think about, how behind the glamour there's a good deal of loneliness.

I'd like to have seen my buddies from home again, but once you're famous your old friends seem to think you're above them or something. I'd like to have got together with them for a beer. I wouldn't have worn my crown or anything. I'd have wanted them to treat me like one of the guys.

Our deadly bread

Overrated Breads of the World:
The Kaiser Roll
(78th in a series)
The first public suggestion that the Kaiser roll was overrated was made at an unruly session of the 16th International Bread Congress in Stuttgart in 1923. Johannes Brinker, the Mad Baker of Lièges, one of the hotheads who survived the 1911 Basel bakeoff, recommended that Sir Ernest (Buns) Staunton-Lind try the tuna salad on a Kaiser that was among the choices in the Stitzplatz cafeteria.

Sir Ernest, in that unthinking way for which he was celebrated (he once fed his mother's entire collection of seventeenth-century toast to gulls on the Strand at Cannes under the impression that he was disposing of the remains of a particularly imprudent breakfast), said anybody who would eat a Kaiser roll would eat the less popular parts of a dromedary.

This so enraged Brinker, an unvarnished Kaiser roll radical, that it was years before he could bring himself to speak civilly to Sir Ernest or to keep from pulling out a Maxim machine gun and mowing down any gathering where he suspected the Briton of being.

So powerful is the Kaiser roll lobby that authorities have for years been hushing up numerous deaths directly attributable to exhaustion and stroke brought on by the effort of eating a Kaiser roll. All twenty-seven contestants in the 1958 Lake Goudge, Minnesota, Kaiser-eating contest died in the course of the event. This was never made public. Most Kaiser-related deaths come after consuming two or three Kaisers, but Mrs. Tina Thompson of Brockville, Ontario, took a fit and passed away after merely seeing a photograph of a ham-and-Swiss on a Kaiser in a neighbour's album.

The Kaiser roll – the original one – was commissioned by Kaiser Wilhelm II of Germany who ordered the court baker to execute "a portrait in bread" that would not only flatter his royal eminence, which the final portrait and all subsequent copies did remarkably, but be a conceptual statement of the toughness and solidity of the man after whom it was fashioned. It is thought that the Kaiser instructed the baker to create a roll that would place him indelibly among the great statesmen of history but that the baker, who came to be regarded as something of a lout, thought he said inedibly.

While North Americans customarily refer to thunder as "God playing at bowls," many eastern Europeans, on hearing thunder, say, "That's God throwing out his Kaiser rolls."

Liver on a Kaiser roll is the provincial sandwich of Manitoba. One pinned to the lapel is a mark of distinction in Winnipeg.

In Andalusia, the Kaiser roll is considered a good luck talisman among girls of marriageable age. They believe that if they fasten a Kaiser roll to their noses with binder twine they will marry Don Jaime, the heir to the vast cork fortune and possessor of a different-coloured Mercedes for every day of the week. Sometimes young Andalusian men laugh and disparagingly refer to an unfortunate prospect as "a two-Kaiser chick," meaning that even with two Kaisers suspended from her nose and a dowry of a million dollars (U.S.) she would be lucky to snare Manuel, the buffoon.

The powerful Kaiser roll lobby frequently firebombs diplomatic functions where they don't serve steak, or even cream cheese for that matter, on a Kaiser while the ambassadors sit around watching the hockey game on TV.

Using laser technology to estimate the number of air holes in a Kaiser roll, Dr. Monica Bender of Princeton University concluded, "a lot." Professor Eugene Ramsay of McGill, in a corroborating paper, placed the figure at "a whole lot. Golly."

Despite constant threats from the powerful Kaiser roll lobby, nutritionists courageously place the nutritional value of a Kaiser roll between that of a parking meter and a dish of bird gravel.

(Next: The Crouton)

Dental hygiene is moral hygiene

There was a businesslike murmuring in the bank, a quiet sound that dropped perceptibly to a strained silence, as one by one, the customers realized a man in a brown ski jacket had a pistol pointed at the teller in the end wicket. She had turned quite pale and was, jerkily, piling money on the counter.

Except for the teller's movements, the scene was as still as a photograph and everyone jumped, startled, when a voice from the back said, crisply, "Excuse me." A slender figure in a white, knee-length clinician's coat began to move through the crowd toward the gunman. "Excuse me, but I'm Cathy, a registered dental hygienist, and just because you lead a busy life is no excuse to neglect your teeth. Open up and let me have a look."

Bewildered, the robber opened up – the note of authority in the voice of a registered dental hygienist is irresistible – and, while he kept his gun trained on the teller, Cathy poked around in his mouth with her mirror and scaling instruments. "Just as I suspected, a goshawful buildup of plaque." She addressed the trembling customers. "Plaque is that gucky substance that accumulates at the base of the teeth, providing a fertile environment for bacteria. It is an invitation to gum disease."

She turned back to the gape-mouthed gunman. "Flossing is essential," she said. "You must make flossing a habit, a normal part of your daily routine, and now is a good time to start."

Pulling a container of floss from her pocket, she offered a length to the robber, who dutifully set to work with it. While his attention was distracted, the hygienist swiftly wound endless filaments of floss around him, binding him with the powerful material until he resembled a cocoon. At that moment, in burst the police, led by Sergeant Nathan Pearlstein of the holdup squad.

"Faith and begorrah," said Sergeant Pearlstein, examining the trussed-up crook, "you've beaten us to the punch again, girl. Sure and it's a fine thing you do for the law-abiding citizens of this fair city. And sure it's a constant wonder to me that nobody has yet penned a book about the exploits of Cathy, the crime-fighting registered dental hygienist. This is the sixth robbery you've foiled this week, saints be praised."

"The seventh, Sergeant," Cathy said modestly, blushing to the roots of her pearly white smile.

Later, in her clinic, Cathy was scraping busily away between a pair of enormous molars attached to the jaws of a fat man who gurgled nervously in her chair. Suddenly, her registered dental hygienist sense began to tingle, a sure sign of trouble.

"What was your name again?" she asked the patient.

"Kkswfggjqsqnknk," he replied.

"Oh, sorry," she said, removing her hands and several steel implements from his mouth. "What was that again?"

"I'm Herbert Trombone, businessman and philanthropist," he said, dabbing at his lips with his green paper bib.

Cathy looked pensively at the illuminated display of Trombone's dental X-rays, then she began to probe inquisitively around in the pulpy mulch of diseased tissue that surrounded his rear-most chompers. Then she whipped out her floss and swiftly crocheted the patient to the reclining chair. "You might be Herbert Trombone, businessman and philanthropist," she said, "but my investigations show you are also Herbert (Herbie the Horn) Trombone, organized criminal, and I'm turning you in."

"Faith and begorrah," said Sergeant Pearlstein, scratching his head as his men frogmarched a subdued Trombone out of Cathy's clinic. "Sure and you've done it again, apprehended yet another mobster in the nick of time, saints be praised. There's no denying that this city would be wide open to the likes of him if it weren't for the efforts of the likes of you. How do you do it, girl?"

"Oh, you could see it yourself, Sergeant, if you were a registered dental hygienist," said Cathy. "People who respect our way of life, who are law-abiding and nice, they care for their teeth. Those who don't – well, tooth decay and moral decay go together."

Depravity of the week

There was a special on television yesterday, a dramatized account of how a decent, respectable boy, as a result of his parents' failure to discipline him, drifted into crime, murdered a pawnbroker, and ended up being executed in the electric chair.

Based on real events, the film contained a special message for young people. The message was that an ordinary, respectable young person who lacks discipline and who strays from the straight and narrow can end up going to the electric chair. It can happen to anybody.

A week before there was another special on television. It was the dramatized account of how a respectable man got caught up in an incestuous relationship with his daughter.

And before that was the special about how child molesters don't always appear to be drooling perverts. Sometimes they are little more than respectable men overcome with an urge to reach out and touch the kid next door.

In both these specials, too, the underlying theme was that whatever was happening could happen to anybody.

This idea that anybody, any ordinary, decent, respectable person at all, can suddenly sink to the absolute depths of depravity has been a godsend for television. Gone is the need for expensive plots with elements in them like greed or ambition or envy or revenge to motivate character. Gone also is the need for villains like J.R. Ewing or The Joker or Dr. Moriarty. This represents a considerable saving.

But it has a downside that makes television executives anxious. Just how many depravities are there for ordinary, respectable people to try their hands at? You might at first think the supply is endless, but in a few seasons of specials you are going to run through all but the most esoteric. Viewers will start to say, "I just plain don't believe a decent, respectable person would do a think like that with the ice cream and the garden hose and the barbershop quartet."

The problem, ultimately, is that while decent, respectable people engaging in depravity might be a slice of life, it is the exact opposite of great drama. Once we get over the novelty of seeing a new depravity every week, it is going to become a big yawn to discover that some colourless lump of ordinary mortality is indulging in it. It will be like watching your neighbour's vacation slides.

What drama demands, and the audience, too, if it is to experience the transport of imagination and the purge of catharsis, is great characters with great twisted reasons for sinking to greater depths than any of us sitting watching can ever aspire to. That is why Oedipus, Richard III, J.R. Ewing are transcendental characters.

But since those characters have been used up or are already under contract, television has decided to plow a new furrow. It plans to stick with depravities, since there are some left to explore, but instead of relying on upright citizens to wallow in them in dramatized accounts, TV will show genuine, twisted criminals carrying out genuine crimes, live, on the home screen.

Since what most of us know about murder or child molesting or incest comes either from news accounts of arrests and trials or from made-for-TV movies, watching a pawnbroker actually be murdered or some actual weirdo offer candy to kids will be an entertainment breakthrough.

It could turn out, though, that watching real criminals perpetrate real crimes will, after a season or two, become as boring as watching make-believe respectable people pretend to be depraved.

Television knows this. That's why it got so excited when it heard about County Court Judge Bruce Hawkins.

Hawkins came up with the engaging idea of crime ratings. If there is anything that commands television's attention it is ratings. Hawkins rated the rape in a case he heard as a 2, on a scale of 1 to 10.

For years television has been filling the sporting void with mock spectacles such as *The Battle of the Network Stars*. Now it could have an honest show that rivalled the Olympics; vicious criminals vying with one another and Judge Hawkins holding up the scores after each performance: 4.7 for bloodiness, 8 for artistic expression, 6.5 for depravity.

Talking turkey

Christmas is creeping up on us again and it's time we gave some serious thought to preparing for one of the most glorious parts of that wonderful annual celebration, Christmas dinner.

I don't care what anybody says, I think tradition has a big role to play in festivals such as Christmas. Tradition helps us feel that we are taking part in something much bigger than might be the case if we judged only by our own table, no matter how gaily decked.

Tradition links us with the past. It means sharing with our neighbours, sharing the important things, sharing feelings and those special holiday thoughts that make the season bright.

For me, Christmas and tradition add up to just one thing when it comes to dinnertime, and that's turkey – turkey with all the trimmings. Some of you may be put off by the size of the task involved in preparing the good old-fashioned turkey dinner. That's why more and more of you are choosing to get by instead with the good old-fashioned bologna sandwich or hot dogs.

Now, some of you are likely saying, what does a bachelor know about creating a truly sumptuous Christmas feast? Bachelors just know about ordering pizza. Well, some bachelors know a thing or two more than that, and here's a sure-fire recipe for a Christmas spread that never fails to make the holiday heart sparkle.

The excitement begins with the shopping expedition. Just entering the grocery store and seeing the tinsel streamers, red and green and gold, dancing on strings between the shelves creates a tingle of merry anticipation and goodwill.

How delicious the goodies look, stacked in the freezer, promising mouth-watering goodness. Just look at the photograph on the package. Beautifully rounded slabs of tender white meat nestling on a savory bed of lovely, browned, crumbly bread stuffing, all steeping in a rich, dark gravy. You almost think you can dip your finger into the picture and dab it succulently on your tongue.

There is a special elegance to the silvery gleam of the plate the turkey comes so conveniently pre-served in. There is a thoughtful, individual section for each part of the dinner, and cleverly crimped edges to keep the portions from spilling out and soiling your placemat.

See the potatoes, whipped and light as cumulus clouds lazing across a carefree sky, and drenched with a fragrant, yellow butter-like substance that looks fresh and inviting. On the other side are the peas and carrots, each pea spring-garden green and juicy and each carrot cut into a cube of unimaginable perfection.

In the middle is the most tantalizing treat of all, beckoning you, calling out to you to rush through all those other mere earthly delights. The splendid square of apple-cranberry cobbler! You thank your stars that you have been good all year so you won't be sent away on this most special day without any dessert.

Back home in the kitchen, everything becomes a flurry of activity. The box is opened and its chill, foil-wrapped contents removed. The oven is preheated to exactly 204 degrees C (440F). This is a terribly important step. If you don't preheat the oven, your dinner will remain frozen solid and you will be forced to chip away at it with a hammer and chisel, all the while weeping those tears that only a cook who has produced a flop can weep.

Next, cut or tear the foil and fold it back to expose the dessert. Ah, the dessert! Imagine it turning crisp and firm, while the ruby sweetness of the cranberry topping soaks into its every pore.

Finally, place it in the oven for thirty minutes.

Thirty minutes. Just the right amount of time to clear the newspapers and laundry and unopened bills off the table and to sponge it off with a J-cloth. At Christmas it is always attractive to use a red or green J-cloth. Glance at the oven from time to time to make sure there is no smoke. Meanwhile, pick a knife and fork out of the sink, run some hot water over them and set the table. Then have a fast snort of something.

Ding! Time is up already! Thankfully, all is ready. Remove your treasure from the oven – carefully, so as not to burn your fingers. Remove the foil and sit down and dig in. Sort of makes you wonder what the poor people are doing.

The wild raspberry caper

The biggest patch of wild raspberries in the city is on the east bank of the Humber River, about a quarter mile south of where Bloor Street crosses. It is south of the jungle, on a neck of land between the river and a broad oval pond that today has the same hazy sheen as the sky and carries instantaneous replays of the clouds.

I discovered the patch on a rainy spring morning when the jungle was at its gloomiest, skinny trees, twisted and bent, black and primitive, draped with vines. Everything wet and snaky. It is impossible to walk through the jungle and not look back over your shoulder every few steps. Unheard things slip along behind you, unseen things grab at your ankles, blind eyes burn holes between your shoulder blades. This is where the goblins dance on nights when the moon is full.

If you make it through the jungle (and I think some don't. Paths often start out bravely, become progressively more narrow and apprehensive, then give up in a weedy tangle), anything you find on the other side will look good. A stand of wild raspberry canes fuzzy with blossoms, the first pale nubbins of unripened fruit showing here and there, looks like a treasure.

Plans were laid then and there for a harvesting expedition. In August. Secrecy was essential. No one else must know where the raspberries were hidden. A map was drawn. X marked the spot.

Then summer came and did what the loveliest of summers do. It filled up with itself and overflowed. Spring's plans drifted away, floated around a bend in the sparkling stream of days, and disappeared from sight, and soon from memory. Until this morning when dawn, for some reason, recalled the raspberries. In the next thing to panic, I dressed and hurried down there, climbed under the bridge, tumbled down the bank, and whipped through the jungle as if it were no more forbidding than a bowling green. All the time I was saying to myself, "Too late! I'm much too late."

And I was. Much too late. The canes were bare, picked clean. I felt the little pang you feel when you see a former lover go by on somebody else's arm. I believe it is called jealousy. It doesn't even matter if it was you who decided to end the affair, there is still that little black pang when you learn she has found unending happiness with someone new.

I looked accusingly around at the big houses on the high bank above the pond. Somewhere, somewhere out there was somebody who had picked my raspberries and found happiness with them. Perhaps it is foolish to feel proprietary about wild things, and then to feel robbed when they disappear, but one of the peculiar things about going off where few others go is that when you discover a secret thing, you feel it is your secret thing and yours alone. I got a tad grumpy.

The thing about nature is that it all makes sense, it can all be explained, from bud to green leaf to the leaves changing colour and falling. You always know where you stand. You can screw nature up, but left to its own devices it performs with reassuring predictability when not much else does.

People don't. We make plans, make promises, then, often as not, change our plans, forget them, break our promises. Come up with something else we'd rather do. Phone and say, "Listen, I'm sorry, but something's come up. . . ." The raspberries behaved exactly as they always have. And I guess I did, too, if you figure that my behaviour is always annoyingly random.

Finding your raspberries picked can leave you with a bleak view of humanity.

I cheered myself up by touching the touch-me-not seedpods of the jewelweed, some of which still bloomed, brilliant pink, in the shadows. When you touch the ripe pod – it is about the size of a cashew – it goes bam! and seeds explode from it like buckshot from a gun.

A flock of white-throated sparrows, northern birds hanging around here until winter, creeping south, drives them once more before it, chittered around me, warning me to get ready, big changes were coming. I'd better start making plans, they said.

At the edge of the pond I watched the two skies. A great blue heron rose from one, wheeled around, and disappeared into the other.

3
Arts and Litter

Country and Proust

This here's the title of a country and western song that I wrote. Wait. Hold everything right there. Get her straight. This here's the title that I wrote of a country and western song. I didn't write no song, just the title. And I don't want you thinking I wrote it by taking pen in hand and staring off into space trying to dream up something to set down, the way you do when you write a letter home. That would be wrong. The title come to me out of the clear blue. That's all there was to it.

That's the way I understand it is with a lot of writers, Marcel Proust for instance. Something comes to them and they set it down. Marcel Proust never wrote no country and western songs that I am aware of, nor titles neither. With a name like Marcel, are you kidding? It's tough enough making it in the country and western music business without dragging along a liability like the name Marcel. "And now, from the stage at Opryland, here's a bright young newcomer to sing a song he wrote of his own composition, Mr. Marcel Proust." Everywhere you looked you'd see folks turning off the radios in their pickup trucks. "I ain't going to sit here and listen to no hairdresser," they'd say.

On top of that, he wrote in French. "Henry, there is some hairdresser named Marcel singing some sort of mumbo-jumbo in a foreign language on the radio."

"Turn it off right away, Joleen. Lord knows what the world is coming to." His standing on the C&W charts would stick at sub-minus below zero.

Fortunately, my title come to me in English, which everybody recognizes is the international language of country and western music. It goes like this: He Don't Mean No Harm, But He Don't Know No Better. I like it, especially because of two things. It's got scope, and it's real long, which is the most important thing of all to consider in a country and western song title.

You go to the discotheque you can hear songs, *entire songs*, that don't have as many words in them as a run-of-the-mill country and western song title, much less a hit. I'm not familiar enough with the business yet to know if it's because country and western title writers get paid so much per word while disco writers just deal dope and don't care how much they get apart from that, or what.

I don't even know if they buy country and western titles or whether you got to have the song to go with them which, as I have already indicated, I have not got. I been hoping that one might come out of the clear blue that would accompany the title and if one does I am prepared to whip it down on paper. So far, nothing. Now that I say that, here comes another title, if that don't beat all. Here it is: A Title's All I Got, The Song Ain't Wrote Yet.

I like that one, too, for the following reasons. It's real long (see above), and it's about country and western music, which is what 90 per cent of country and western songs are about. I don't know why that is, either, unless maybe there's just plain no market for a country and western song about punk rock music or *Swan Lake* or the like.

You would have to study the market to know for sure and studying the market ain't my specialty. My specialty, in case it hasn't occurred to you, is these titles that keep coming out of the clear blue. It Just Occurred To Me That It Didn't Occur To You. How do you like that one? Well, you can't expect all winners off the bat. Some you got to polish up a little.

If there's big money to be made in country and western titles, it would be real gratifying as I appear gifted that way while some are not gifted in titles any way you look at it. Marcel Proust for instance. Here is what he called his biggie: *A la Recherche du Temps Perdu*. What on earth do you suppose he was driving at? He should of took it to a title specialist.

A title specialist would of took one look at it and said, "Marcel, what you should call your book is *The Betsy By Harold Robbins*. That is a good title because a) people will think your book was wrote by Harold Robbins which they like because he writes mainly about people having sex with each other and b) by the time they get home from the newsstand with it and discover it's in French and was written by a hairdresser, it'll be too late."

Mr. Bone and the fossil hunters

The Garden Gate Book Company, otherwise known as the Grade 2-and-3 class at Garden Avenue Public School, Dan Bone teacher and publisher, has so far published several books on their word processor. Some of the titles are *The Frog and the Fly, I Saw a Raccoon, Oscar the Snake,* and *The Transformers.* One day this week they collected material for a book about a hike to High Park, which is not far from the school, and to Sunnyside Beach, with special attention to be paid to fossils and seagulls and kite-flying.

Here are some related incidents:

The day began in Room 207 with everybody in a state of high anticipation. There was "O Canada," then Mr. Bone, in a blue shirt with "I'm for the birds" written on the front, read a Haida Indian prayer that began, "O good sun, look thou down upon us. Shine, shine upon us." Then the incubator was filled with eggs that will hatch in three weeks, and we set off. The prayer worked perfectly. The sun shone, shone upon us.

On the way to High Park, Jennifer said, "Miss Porter's class isn't coming, and I'm glad. They came last time and they spoiled everything. They made us lose one of our kids." Losing a kid is bad form. To prevent such a thing, Mr. Bone arranged for a police escort across Parkside Drive. Part of the police escort was a big, brown-dappled police horse named Billy. People in Grades 2 and 3 are exceptionally good patters, as Billy found out.

Everybody explored a valley Mr. Bone called Chipmunk Valley. There was one chipmunk, but there were two snakes and two dead squirrels. A better name would be Snakes and Dead Squirrels Valley. One of the snakes was a beauty, a yard long and an inch in diameter, a garter snake. It was particularly admired by Bronson, who captured it, and by Chris, who stashed it in his lunch bag. All this was too much for the snake, which whoopsed its breakfast, which consisted mainly of dew worms. This caused a sensation among a number of kids who came to the mistaken conclusion that the snake had just had a bunch of babies amidst Chris's lunch. When Mr. Bone caught wind of the affair he became cross and delivered a stern lecture on leaving wild creatures alone and how if any of the kids happened to get captured by a whole bunch of giant snakes, they would whoops their breakfasts, too.

While crossing Lake Shore Boulevard all the change fell out of Damien's pocket. Mr. Bone made everybody stay well back while he went to rescue the money. He was nearly run over many times. Losing an adult on a research expedition is an occupational hazard.

Carly said her Indian name was Running Deer and that her ancestors lived in the woods where they hunted and fished. Maybe that's why she was such a good fossil hunter. She found what Jennifer was positive was a dinosaur bone. Dinosaur bones apparently look like very hard pancakes. Carly said it would bring a lot of money at the museum. The kids described fossils as "dead fish in stones." Keith found a stone that was chock full of dead fish. He passed his prize around, but there was a moment's confusion and Stephen, not realizing he had been handed Keith's prize fossil, used it as a skipping stone. Stephen is one of the better stone-skippers in the class.

The visiting seagull expert set up his telescope so the kids could look at the gulls on the breakwater and see that there were at least two different kinds of gulls in the world, ring-billed and herring. To the visiting seagull expert's horror, two ring-billed gulls became very affectionate – actually they became totally affectionate – while Chris was watching through the telescope. The expert's hope that Chris, who was only eight, would miss the significance of what he was seeing and think he was just watching some curious seagull game went down in flames when Chris turned to his little friends and announced, "These seagulls are making sex, one on top of each other. Do you want to have a look?" The seagull expert snatched away his telescope and retreated, shaken.

The expedition ended back at the school with the proper number of kids and, surprisingly, the proper number of adults, some of whom had gained a much deeper appreciation of life. It should make for a good book, a best-seller at least.

The snows of Hemingway

A young woman I know, a university student, has just returned from two months in Africa. During her visit she climbed Mount Kilimanjaro. The climb took three and a half days. There were fifteen in her party when they started up. Of those, eight gave up along the way. She was one of the seven who made it to the summit.

Because of the cold, the thin air, and the footing – it is a steep, scree slope, gravel and loose rocks that keep giving way – it took six hours to negotiate the last three and a half kilometres. She came away from the experience with a wrenched knee, two toes that are still numb, mild surprise at her own endurance, and exhilaration from the sheer splendidness of it all.

"Did you see the leopard up there?" I asked.

"Leopard?" she said. "What leopard? There were no leopards up there."

When she said that I realized just how dead Ernest Hemingway was. I dug it out and read it to her. From *The Snows of Kilimanjaro*. "Kilimanjaro is a snow-covered mountain 19,710 feet high, and is said to be the highest mountain in Africa. Its western summit is called by the Masai 'Ngaje Ngai,' the House of God. Close to the western summit there is the dried and frozen carcass of a leopard. No one has explained what the leopard was seeking at that altitude."

"It's 19,740 feet high. He got that wrong," she said with the assurance of someone who has been there and taken its measure.

Poor old Hemingway. All he'd really wanted was to become immortal and here was one more indication that he'd blown it. He had believed that if he wrote down what he really felt, rather than what he was supposed to feel, then he would have captured "the real thing, the sequence of motion and fact which made the emotion and which would be as valid in a year or in ten years or, with luck and if you stated it purely enough, forever."

And here a youthful student of literature comes down from his mountain and doesn't know about his leopard.

I imagine someone someday asking her if the earth moved and her saying, "What's that supposed to mean?"

What is touching about all this is that hardly twenty years ago I was using Hemingway, more precisely using what he wrote, as a model for how to live the right sort of life. He foresaw what came to be called "situational ethics." He wrote, "I know only that what is moral is what you feel good after and what is immoral is what you feel bad after." That sounded utterly jaded and profound. I memorized the words and quoted them in endless conversations in student coffee shops.

He also provided me with a model as a writer. Not his style, although with almost everybody my age I mimicked it for a while, until it became a parody of what proved to be Hemingway's own unfortunate self-parody. They were there for the fishing, for the fishing and the hunting and the drinking and the love-making. For the definite article. Was it good? It was good.

Actually, it wasn't all that great. But Hemingway did challenge me to set down "the good and the bad, the ecstasy, the remorse and sorrow, the people and the places and how the weather was. If you can get so that you can give that to people, then you are a writer."

It is one thing Hemingway wrote that I still believe.

My heart broke for the hopeless love between Jake Barnes and Lady Brett Ashley. Perhaps it was an odd thing to fantasize yourself as a hero who had suffered "the ultimate wound," but there you are. I did. I saw myself run before the bulls at Pamplona and idolized his tacky bullfighters and his sad soldiers and his seedy boxers. In all of them he looked for that wonderful commodity, "grace under pressure." I was sure there was no better quality a man could have.

Courage was never more perfectly described than in *The Old Man and the Sea*. He struggled to land the fish all the while thinking that if the Great DiMaggio could persevere with a bone spur on his heel, then what was happening to one inconsequential old man was nothing.

I could go on. I won't.

I asked the young woman for more details of her climb. She told me. It sounded like a fine adventure.

T for two

Sunday. Rain. Bathurst and Bloor. Honest Ed's. In the corner window, Mr. T, a large, black television character who has a strange haircut and who wears enough gold and diamonds to sink Zsa Zsa Gabor and who is revered by people who believe violence is justified if it all works out for the best, is to meet his fans and sign his books. Keep this in mind as we examine . . .

Sunday. Rain. Markham Street, around the corner from Honest Ed's. David Mirvish's bookstore, David Mirvish being the son of Honest Ed. In an upstairs corner, Timothy Findley, a medium-sized, white Canlit character who has grey, professorial hair and who wears wire-rimmed spectacles and who is revered by people who believe there is such a thing as Canlit, is to meet his fans and sign his books. Coincidence?

When Mr. T appears in the window, his fans, several many thousand strong and soaking wet, push and shove and jam the street, disrupting traffic and behaving in a semi-riotous manner. Timothy Findley's fans are nowhere apparent. But perhaps that is because Findley is not at the moment apparent, either. In fact, *Findley does not appear to sign his books until Mr. T stops signing his books and disappears into hiding.* Coincidence?

The authorities claim Mr. T stole away early, and disappointed his several many thousand soggy fans, because Mr. T was afraid the semi-riot would turn into the genuine article. Other authorities claim that Findley was late showing up to greet his fans *because he had trouble getting through the semi-riot around the corner.* Coincidence?

If that doesn't tell you something, consider this for a capper: Mr. T's last name, T, is composed (in its entirety) of the same letter as the first letter of Findley's first name, Timothy. Put it all together and you begin to smell one very big mixed-media hoax.

Possibility 1. Mr. T is really a mild, bookish, white guy who, to make a buck, dolls himself up as a tough, flashy, black guy and goes around killing and maiming and being sanctimonious.

Possibility 2. Timothy Findley is really a tough, flashy, black guy who puts on whiteface and lets the air out of his biceps and triceps and ego and passes himself off as a mild, bookish, white guy, thus gaining some peace and obscurity.

Possibility 3. There is no real Findley or real Mr. T. They are publicity gimmicks dreamed up by Honest Ed, who needs a publicity gimmick every week or he goes into withdrawal.

Item: The same person who decorates Ed's stores obviously decorated Mr. T.

Item: Ed's quest for respectability (in this town you'd think it was enough to call yourself "Honest") led him to shore up the Royal Alex and London's Old Vic; why not, likewise, a Canadian author, which are such respectable things that the government often gives them grants to keep them going.

Item: Did Mr. T appear in Simpson's window? Did Findley appear in a back corner of Cole's?

Mr. T and Findley have a suspicious number of things in common. Findley wrote a novel called *The Wars.* Mr. T is a war.

Findley's book, *Famous Last Words,* caused a scandal because it was a fiction that maintained the Duke and Duchess of Windsor were part of a Nazi plot to overthrow King George VI. Mr. T's book, *Mr. T, The Man With The Gold*, an autobiography, caused a scandal because members of his family claim it is a fiction, period. "We look on the book as being a complete lie," said sister Angie.

Finally, there is a new cereal on the shelves called "Mr. T." There is no cereal called Timothy Findley, but it is estimated that a page from one of his books, shredded into a bowl with milk and sugar, has the same nutritional value.

Whoever is responsible for the hoax included some red herrings to throw off all but the shrewdest investigator: the police had to contain Mr. T's mob; the police did not have to contain Findley's mob, which, at times, numbered nine. Such ruses were transparent.

How the Findley fanatics and the Mr. T maniacs will react now that they learn they have been duped and that their heroes are one and the same, or possibly neither, remains to be seen.

But that's their problem.

J.D. is a pest

J.D. Salinger dropped by the house the other night. We were just sitting down to eat. "Hi," he said. "Hope I haven't caught you at a bad time. Happened to be in the neighbourhood and thought I'd stop in and say hello. Cold, isn't it? God, it's cold! Didn't think my car would start, but it started. Oops! I've tracked snow on your carpet. What a mess! Should have taken off my boots. What's that great smell? Shepherd's pie? It's not your dinner time is it? God, I love shepherd's pie. What? Oh, no. I couldn't. Well, if you insist."

J.D. Salinger is getting to be a pest.

That was the second time in a week he happened to be in the neighbourhood at dinner time. The time before it was pork chops and scalloped potatoes. God, he loves pork chops and scalloped potatoes.

I never laid eyes on J.D. Salinger in my life until two weeks ago. I'd been to the dentist and I'm coming down on the elevator and this guy gets on. Tall, grey-haired guy with kind of a beaky nose, kind of stoop-shouldered. "Hi," he said. Right away I figure we've landed a weirdo, anybody says "Hi" when he gets on the elevator. "Hi, I'm J.D. Salinger. Call me Jerry. What's your name?"

And he goes around to everybody on the elevator introducing himself and everybody has this expression like when your underwear has just turned to ice cream and shrunk a couple sizes.

When the elevator stops, there's a terrific stampede to get off and I go into this bar to have a snifter before going back to the office and I look up and who's standing right there beside me with a smile on him like half a Cadillac hubcap? Good old Jerry. I jumped. "Hi," he said. "Remember me? We just met on the elevator. This sure is a nice place. What's that you're drinking? Let me buy you one. Sure is a nice day. This beer tastes great. God, I love meeting new people, finding out what they think about things. Sure is a shame about the Leafs, isn't it?"

And on he went. You ever been in that situation? Some guy comes up to you and starts to talk like a maniac and won't shut up and you figure there's no way of getting rid of him short of strangling him?

"You maybe heard the name before?" he said. "J.D. Salinger?"

I told him I thought it was the same as the name of the guy who wrote *Catcher In The Rye*. The recluse. Lives somewhere in New England. "New Hampshire," he said. "Cornish, New Hampshire. That's me. I'm the one. So you heard of me? That's great. You know, you write all those books and you wonder if anybody remembers. You sit there all day writing, thinking maybe nobody cares. You feel cut off. That's why I like to get out. See what's happening. You can't live in a vacuum. So, listen, what do you think of my stuff?"

It was my round. I told him it was a long time since I'd read anything by him, and my memory wasn't all that hot anyway.

"Neither's mine," he said. "Funny how some stuff you remember and some you don't. *The Catcher In The Rye* is what most people remember. It was about that kid, Holden Caulfield. About him leaving school. God, what a dope that kid was. Then I wrote about that Glass family, Franny and Zooey and their jerk brother. What was his name? Sidney? Sheldon? Something like that. I couldn't stand him. I had him commit suicide. It was the only way to get rid of him. He was driving me nuts. What an egomaniac that guy was."

I had to leave, but, not thinking too clearly, I gave him my card. He called me at the office. Wanna go for a drink after work? Wanna catch a movie? Let's get together and shoot the breeze. How long did I think it would take the Leafs to rebuild? He'd phone four, maybe five times a day. Show up just when it was time to go for lunch. "God, it's good to see you," he'd say. "What's new? Wait'll I tell you what happened to me today." And you'd get the whole thing. What he had for breakfast. Who he met on the street.

It was one in the morning. "God, it's one in the morning," he said. "I'd better let you folks get some shut-eye. Thanks for the shepherd's pie. Let's get together for lunch. Nighty-night."

As we climbed into bed, my wife said, "God, I thought he'd never leave."

"You thought who'd never leave?" said J.D. Salinger.

Send no money

This chain essay comes to you for good luck. Everywhere it has been read it has caused good luck. The original copy is in a cannister in the vault of a chartered bank. The cannister is watertight. You will receive good luck within four (4) days of reading this essay providing you do not break the chain. THIS IS NOT A JOKE. You will receive the good luck in the mail postage-paid. Or maybe by courier. Marie Lefebvre found some on the sidewalk.

Read this essay if you need good luck. DO NOT SEND MONEY for faith has no price on it. This is first chain essay ever. Powerful forces are working. Do not disregard and stack with the papers by the door for the Wednesday pickup of bundled materials. Carry in wallet or reticule if possible.

Take note of the following: Evelyn Bosco failed to read the essay and a big thing fell out of the sky and landed on her. Arthur Ramirez was a busy executive and glanced only at the front cover and the contents page. His secretary read this essay at lunch and THAT VERY AFTERNOON told Ramirez of the ease with which she could provide certain information to Ramirez's wife and the tax department. She has been living high off the hog since.

DO NOT BREAK THE CHAIN. After a few days you will receive a surprise. This is true even if you are not superstitious. Reverend Howard Flinder read this essay from the pulpit of Knox Presbyterian Church and THE VERY NEXT DAY was promoted to Archbishop of Canterbury. Numerous such instances abound.

While stationed in Labrador Sergeant Albert Gilhooley did not read this essay and all his hair fell out everywhere. After retirement in Tempe, Arizona, he bought twenty copies of this essay and delivered them to neighbours. THAT NIGHT interstellar voyagers carried Gilhooley to a planet where hair is no object. It will work if chain is not broken. If twenty copies bought and delivered to neighbours so much the better. Copies available at bookstores today.

RESULTS MANY TIMES GUARANTEED. Mary Johnstone did not read this essay and fell in an excavation. Yen Chow Kue of the Far East did not read this essay and furze destroyed his rice crop. This essay was written by monks in prehistoric times and found in a locker in the Chicago bus station. Translated by myself it is offered to you for luck. Ferdinand Johanssen made of it a needlepoint sampler and THE VERY NEXT MORNING found his basement drain unclogged. This is a numerous occurrence.

It is wasting this essay to deliver to people who don't need good luck. Rattman Hutterjeet sent it to a wealthy millionaire who lived in a mansion but the laundry lost his dhoti nevertheless. A physician in Egypt delivered it to a man on skidrow and WITHIN WEEKS a lord from England proclaimed the man his long-lost heir and wept openly. There are likewise numerous instances here.

Do not change this essay. A curse is between the lines if changed. A Dutch sea captain changed all the verbs to something or other and was SOON THEREAFTER arrested for golfing nude in a former protectorate. Do not stop reading once started. DeWayne C. Simpson stopped reading after the second paragraph. THAT VERY MINUTE he was called to the phone and told that due to failure to pay a hospital bill his appendix would be put back in.

Send no money. Buy twenty copies for neighbours and friends you have a good feeling toward. YOU ARE UNDER NO OBLIGATION except bad luck frequently befalls if you break the chain. No man who became the president of any non-Communist nation ever broke the chain. It is just coincidence? Do a favour for yourself.

Nothing bad has happened to Philip Escobar since he read this essay even though many individuals are seeking to push his face in. But his VERY OWN BROTHER was a playboy and thought this essay of no personal use so did not read it and soon had to stay home because mice nested in his shoes. There are many numerous instances such as these.

Luck will flow if read. Do not break the chain. SEND NO MONEY.

Morning men

It's seven a.m. in Metro, folks, and here's Vinny with the news.

Thanks, Grant. Good morning, folks. Vinny here with the news. But first, here's Merle with the traffic.

Morning, everybody. I'll have a complete rundown on the traffic situation right after we hear from Phil with the weather.

Hi, Merle. You're looking great this morning, kid, and what a morning! I'll fill you in on the details as soon as we hear from Fran on the entertainment beat.

Thanks, old buddy. Fran here, folks, with the latest on the bright lights and a whole lot of things to do and see in the coming week. What a week! I'll tell you all about it when Merle finishes the traffic.

Fran, uh, excuse me, folks. This is Vinny with the news. Fran, you're supposed to go back to Phil with the weather.

Wait, Vinny. Excuse me. Good morning, folks. This is Chuck with the sports and the latest rundown on scores from around the league. I thought Fran with entertainment was supposed to go first to Chuck with sports and then I would be right back with details after Merle wrapped up the weather.

Wrong, guys, just hold everything for a second. This is Merle and I don't have the weather. I have the traffic and Fran with entertainment was supposed to come back to Merle with traffic, then after I filled the folks in on all the earlier accidents we go back to Phil with the news.

Phil doesn't do the news, Merle. Remember me? I'm Vinny with the news. Phil does a rundown on whether the trains are on schedule and whether there are delays on airline flights and then we hear from Marv on entertainment, then Fran does the time, then it's over to me.

Over your head is more like it, Vinny. I do the time. I say, Morning folks, Grant here. It's 7:15. Then I spin the platters.

The Platters! That's about your speed, you neanderthal. Listen, nobody would listen to a station that had Mumbles McDodo as morning man if it wasn't for my newscast. So keep your trap shut. Now, all right, Fran, you finish up the sports and then go back to Merle with the weather.

I don't have the sports, Vinny, I have the entertainment. I think Marv has the sports and we get to him right after Chuck updates yesterday's stock market closings. Let's try it this way: Chuck with markets, Marv with sports, me with entertainment, Fran with weather, Merle with traffic and – I think I must have missed somebody. Who has the train and airline schedules?

Who's this Marv guy, anyway? I'd like to meet him. I don't even think we do markets on this show. I'm Chuck with sports and after sports I'm going to Phil with weather and I don't much care what the rest of you do.

Not till after the earlier accidents, jocknose.

You are an earlier accident, Merle. Phil here with the weather, folks. Before I go any further, I'd like to say a word about guys sneaking onto another guy's turf. Yesterday that idiot clown Chuck said the ball game was rained out. Rain is my beat and I'd appreciate if he'd stay off it. How would he feel if I started giving horseracing scores?

Cheesed off, Phil, just the way I feel when a creepo like Fran tries to muscle in and say who's going to do what on my newscast. I'm the newscaster. I've got the big stories of the day from Iran and Persia and Asia Minor, the stories that will shape this day in the pages of history, and now I sit and listen while some boy soprano tries to take over. I'll tell you where to put your bright lights, Fran.

You're an egomaniac, you know. The only reason we have even a single listener is because people want to know if they're stuck in traffic. They want to hear Merle, the Traffic Goddess.

Get stuffed, you whiny broad. Now back to Vinny with the news.

Nice try, Vinny, but too late. Morning, folks. It's 7:15 and old Grant here has your favourite music. Stay tuned till eight for a complete rundown of news, weather, sports, and everything else going on in the big town today.

The great art doors

As we grow (let's not mince words) older we find that we shed some of our dreams, some of our ideals, and adopt a view of the world in which the mountains are less lofty, the seas less deep. But if the sun no longer shines so brightly, neither is the night so dark and full of dragons.

If we no longer laugh so readily, neither do our hearts break so easily. If we are no longer so quick on our feet, neither are we so eager to rush in where angels fear to tread. If we no longer crow over our successes, neither do we have to be put together by all the king's men after we fall.

This is maturity. This is the flowering of the seeds of wisdom that were planted in the giddy spring of youth, of careless youth and love. This is accepting ourselves for what we are. This is living the life and not grieving because the dream was not made flesh. This is finding our reach no longer exceeds our grasp.

Thus it is that I have been able to find comfort and have not been downcast by my failure to fulfil my greatest ambition – to find the artist who designed the original "St. Francis of Assisi Preaching To The Birds" aluminum combination storm and screen door. Now that I am (not to mince words) older, I can live with it.

The "St. Francis of Assisi Preaching To The Birds" aluminum combination storm and screen door is, to my taste, the ultimate expression, the apotheosis, if that is the correct word, or whatever the correct word is if it's not, of aluminum combination storm and screen door art, so casually dismissed by critics as "front-porch hardware," and lumped by the catalogues in the lowest of low-brow districts, where reside aluminum siding, eavestroughing, and roofing supplies.

Too many of us, when we think of aluminum combination storm and screen door art, if we think beyond the mindless, abstract curlicues of bent aluminum strips that, had we only the ears to hear, have so much to say about the imaginative sterility of our age, or of whatever age we are prepared to admit to, if we think beyond those, think of the traditional "Battling Stallions," which depicts stallions, heated with lust, reared back on their hind legs, battling, or of "Mallards Taking Wing In A Marsh," which depicts mallards taking wing in a marsh. The one or the other. Together they are said to comprise the gamut of traditional aluminum combination storm and screen door art.

Then one day an artist labouring over his forms in an aluminum foundry had a vision that would reshape the artistic universe. I think of it as a moment that compares with the moment Desi Arnaz first imagined that music that became, for all the world to hear, the mambo; or when Pablo Picasso lit up everybody's life by drawing that very first Happy Face (it was originally in a painting titled "Guernica," but Picasso had second thoughts and replaced it with a horse's head, something he would live to regret).

It was a simple scene, a monk, St. Francis, with tonsured hair, wearing a cassock, or a hassock, whichever it is they wear, with his head cocked back beatifically and one arm eloquently stretched toward a branch upon which were perched a flock of birds, all of them listening raptly to his words.

Creative lightning had struck. Soon a few select aluminum products outlets were retailing the doors and a few fortunate people were purchasing them. Alas, a tragic lacuna, whatever that might be, in the history of artistic expression: there is no record of whom, or perhaps who, it was that was struck by lightning.

It was my ambition, a simple one I thought at first, to rescue this artist from the most abject obscurity and write his name across the firmament in letters of fire so that all might recognize his achievement. I would ask him which other artists had influenced his work (Giotto? Walter Lantz?). I would ask him what his next major work might be ("The Expulsion From The Garden"? "The Second Epistle To The Corinthians"? "The Babylonian Captivity"?).

I made some phone calls, but nobody knew who he was. So the hell with it. I've got better things to do.

Is Mick Jagger smart?

Is Mick Jagger smart? People always point out that Mick Jagger is smart. Nobody ever points out that Billy Joel is smart or Rod Stewart or Neil Young, for that matter. But they always point out that Mick Jagger is. Is he really? Consider the evidence.

The square records fiasco: Mick Jagger was worried that round records took up too much space. He correctly calculated that a square record with the same surface area would fit in a record sleeve of considerably smaller dimensions. A square design would permit people, especially those with large record collections, to own more records – which would mean an increase in profits to the recording industry and to recording artists – or, alternatively, they could use the extra space for house plants or throw rugs to make their surroundings cheerier and increase their listening pleasure.

Mick Jagger had his next LP produced on a square "disc" and other artists, acutely aware of the listening public's hunger for spatial economies, quickly followed suit. Old recordings were reissued on square records and many listeners replaced their entire collections with the new versions.

The recording industry reported unprecedented profits and stocks in house-plant and throw-rug concerns surged, driving market averages up.

But the market collapsed after record buyers attempted to play the square records on their record players. Needles whisked off when they failed to negotiate the right-angle bends in the new grooves and record surfaces became hopelessly scratched; expensive styluses were ruined when they dug into the rubber mats on the turntables and were whacked by the revolving rectangular corners, and tone arms were bent badly out of shape.

Mick Jagger's brainstorm, although he continued to insist it had been a valuable experiment, left a bad taste in the mouths of many members of the listening public.

The skill-testing question controversy: Mick Jagger was listening to the radio one day when the announcer said the first person to call the station would receive, free, a copy of Volume 18 – SO-SZ – of the World Book Encyclopedia. SO-SZ was an intellectual realm where Mick Jagger found himself invariably embarrassed. The night before he had sat silent and red-faced in the pub, contributing nothing while the conversation ranged over South Dakota, Spinoza, spiders, spiritualism, Stalin, and Swaziland. The radio offer was the opportunity he had been longing for.

With dexterity he dialed the station and, to his delight, was the first caller. The station told him, however, that in keeping with broadcasting regulations, they must ask a skill-testing question. In five seconds he must divide 29,836,080 by 912. In scarcely a second Mick Jagger answered 32,715.

Later, following an investigation into questionable dealings in the recording industry, it was revealed that the combination to Mick Jagger's bicycle lock was 32-7-15.

Did Mick Jagger actually do the long-division in his head or did he merely glance at his wrist, where he keeps the combination written in ballpoint, and blurt it out, to profit from a lucky coincidence? Doubt remains in the minds of many members of the listening public, even though Mick Jagger voluntarily submitted to blind tests where he successfully divided 29,836,080 by 912 with his hands tied behind his back.

The secret messages: Satanism or poor recall? When Mick Jagger's records are played backward, an ethereal voice can be heard saying such things as "Mow the lawn," "Clean the eavestroughs," and "Put out garbage." These have been interpreted as demonic messages and the directions are assiduously followed by devil worshippers, who purchase Mick Jagger's records in great numbers and end up living in particularly well-kept dwellings.

Some members of the listening public believe Mick Jagger is cashing in on the religious beliefs of unsuspecting Satanists simply to make money and to keep his neighbourhood tidy, a shrewd double benefit. Others believe that Jagger has such a terrible memory this is the only way he can keep track of his household chores.

Is Mick Jagger smart? Judge for yourself.

Waiting for Waterloo

When the intermission came halfway through the movie *Napoleon* – Napoleon had just broken the siege of Toulon – I was sure it was years since I had stretched my legs. "You'll make it, old-timer," my wife said as we limped to the foyer, which was crowded with people in various sorts of thrall to the silent spectacular. I fetched us drinks.

"What do you think of it so far?" I asked.

"It's kind of overwhelming," she said. "It's hard to imagine a director having such a modern grasp of movement and technique in – when was it made? 1927?"

The crowd shifted around us. "There was a note in the mail from Marci," she said. Marci was our oldest grandchild. Her father had been transferred from seats near us to Row T during the scene when Napoleon first saw Josephine. "Her birthday is soon."

"She'll be a teen-ager," I said. "Too bad they sit so far away."

I remember the moment Marci was born. Some things stay with you – and becoming a grandparent stays. It is like a telegram from God. "You are getting old stop."

Stop. I wish I could.

She was born during the terrible storm when Napoleon was fleeing from his home in Corsica. The revolution he tried to ignite there had fizzled and he put to sea in a tiny boat with only the French Tricolor for a sail. It was intercut with stormy scenes of the beginning of the Reign of Terror in Paris.

An usher came down the aisle and tapped me on the shoulder. "It's a girl," he whispered. People around us in the audience turned and offered congratulations. I squeezed my wife's hand and she went back to be with our daughter and the new baby, who were in Row M.

Then – a sequential flashback – I remembered the birth of our own daughter, Jennifer. There had been a storm then, too. A terrible snowstorm and the young Napoleon was forced by his schoolmaster to sleep outside during it.

It was punishment for fighting with his schoolmates. And as Napoleon lay there, curled up on a cannon, his pet eagle flew down and landed beside him – the eagle of destiny, if you go in for symbolism. At that instant the doctor turned from his labours – and my wife's – and said, "A girl. Congratulations." He got out of my seat – we sat in Row G then – still do – so I could sit down and comfort my family. People around us in the audience offered congratulations.

I passed out cigars and poured champagne for my wife and we cried and laughed and reminisced about how it all began. It all began with a single ticket I had to *Napoleon* and my seat happened to be in Row K beside a lovely girl with corn-coloured hair.

During the snowball fight at the young Napoleon's school, where the future emperor shows his mettle by beating a much bigger army of boys, I introduced myself to the girl with the corn-coloured hair and we got talking. Maybe it was fate? Anyway, we discovered a shared love for destiny and symbolism.

Toward the end of the snowball fight, we were dating steadily. I proposed when Napoleon stepped forward as the schoolyard victor, blood streaming from his eyebrow. She accepted and her parents approved – she was sitting with her parents – and her father threw a lavish wedding for us during the classroom scene where Napoleon seethes when the schoolmaster belittles Corsica.

All the people around us in the audience attended and it was quite a whoop-up, dancing and lots of wine. My bride and I slipped away to a couple of seats in Row J and spent our honeymoon watching Napoleon sing the "Marseillaise" and we nibbled one another's ears and giggled romantically about symbolism and destiny.

I blinked and rubbed my eyes. The crowd in the foyer shifted into focus. "I wish Tommy would call," I said. Tommy. Our son. A bit footloose, but basically a nice kid. The last time we heard he was off living it up with a noisy bunch in Row R.

"He'll settle down one day," my wife said. "Don't worry."

Bells started to ring and we limped back to our seats.

The theatre lights dimmed. I squeezed my wife's hand.

"At least we've got each other," I said.

"And the whole rest of the movie to live," she said.

Following the leaves

In the night it sounded like rushing water, a torrent hissing past the window, but it wasn't water, it was legions of dry leaves scuttling along the pavement, being hurried toward winter by the wind.

There is no call for hurrying. Winter will soon enough be here. You can tell by the frost on your pumpkin; you can tell by how hard it is to get your heart to turn over in the morning; you can tell because the red has gone from the ravines and the baseball news from the sports pages.

Dawn brought a scatter of rain, but the wind dried the leaves, then raced between the apartment buildings, raising brown and gold cyclones that whizzed against the upper storeys.

In Zen, the first priest says, "The leaves are moving." The second priest says, "The wind is moving." The third says, "Not the leaves, not the wind; mind is moving."

Riding the wind above the trees that swayed atop the banks, a hawk, a big one, patrolled ahead as I followed on the stillness of the path that rolled under the Glen Cedar Bridge, meandering along the ravine bottom. Stalks of dry grass clicked together like aunts knitting in another room; bullrushes on the marshy verges had burst and grown grey beards; the thistles were wrinkled, their cheeks caved in. They nodded, lost in memory.

The osmotic shock of turning so suddenly fanciful had knocked the red maples right out of the picture. The birches were bare, too, and some of the willows. But the oaks were pompous as bank directors, dripping dark bronze, russet and plush. The maples that had turned yellow were hopelessly giddy, ringing the chromatic changes from amber up through such brilliant canary that they made a goldfinch that flipped across my path look downright dowdy.

This ravine must have been a glacial stream, and a vigorous one, to judge by how sharply it cut its inside banks as it swirled south. A businesslike stream, gone out of business.

Near a spot on one of the high curves is a house I remember, tucked back from the edge, where a few years ago some people tried to be a family and failed. He hadn't grown up, she had. He thought hawks drifted on the wind for nothing more than the thrill of it; she knew the hawks were working to stay alive. The expert said, "You talk to one another, I know that. But what you say and what you mean are two different things."

And so the conversation ended. The hawk, somewhere near the Bathurst bridge, found work in the trees and disappeared.

The path curved to the right and I spotted a sprawling garden on a terrace in the no-man's-land outside some backyard fences. It was a vegetable garden, a pirate garden, well tended and now carefully roto-tilled by someone I suspect travels a long, stealthy way to get to it. The soil was dark and rich. Dozens of long-used tomato stakes were neatly stacked, waiting for next year. Whoever keeps this garden intends to be back.

The air in the ravine bottom smelled warm and brown, smelled like nutmeg in a Christmas kitchen. I startled a flock of robins, about twenty of them, young males who were playing tag across the path and in the saplings along the brook, loitering.

The path rose toward Heath Street and the subway station and the St. Michael's College School playing field, then down again beyond St. Clair to the city. I turned and made my way back up the ravine and came upon Robert Frost, who had stopped in the lee of the bridge to admire the trees and have a smoke.

"You were wondering," he said, "about how it is when you say one thing and mean another. I remember one time I was setting down some lines about two roads diverging in a yellow wood. One was all jammed with traffic and I was late for dinner. So I took the one that was less-travelled. And, so far as it came to whether I got my dinner or not, it made all the difference.

"Sometimes when there is a difference between what you say and what you mean, it is a disaster. But sometimes it is poetry."

Then he winked and said, "And sometimes you just can't tell."

4
Sports Snorts

Off my game

Lee Trevino and Pete Rose are elderly gentlemen, not unlike myself, who still happen to be at the tops of their games, unlike myself. Lee Trevino can hit the long ball, Pete Rose can run the bases. Each has, within the last while, taken a little, bitty new wife and doing so has given each of them a shot in the arm.

I broached the subject to my wife. She was pouring kibble into a bowl. The dog stood beside her expectantly, knowing that this meant he would soon get his dinner. "Would you say I was a little off my game?" I asked. She set the kibble in front of me and went to the fridge for a steak for the dog. "It's been a while since I could hit the long ball. I no longer move along the base paths like greased lightning."

The dog made a mewling, whiny noise. "Stop begging!" my wife yelled. "You've got your own dinner." I explained that I wasn't begging. I was just checking to see if the dog's steak was done the way he likes it. He likes it medium. I left the table and went back to my kibble.

"You know," I said, "sometimes a person who's off his game needs a shot in the arm." She didn't say anything. She was at the sink peeling running shoes. She likes to peel them and leave them to soak overnight before stuffing them with shavings and baking them. I thought about my career.

I have always been career-oriented. It was a path I chose, rather than becoming hobby-oriented or booze-and-partying-oriented, or oriented toward fast cars and racy women and winning big on the tables at Vegas. It seemed to suit me. I will always cherish the words of my careers adviser in high school, "I advise you to get a career," he said.

I grabbed the first career that came along, and I worked at it, especially while I was in the minors. I polished my short game, tried to keep my head down, learned what I could from the gruff but kindly old supervisors and – sure – got a taste of cynicism from veterans whose careers had slumped and were back in the minors, full of bitterness and tiredness and whisky.

But I punched my card and kept my clients happy and my nose clean and finally I got a shot at the big leagues. I wasn't anything special, not a bonus-baby or anything like that. Oh, I had a desk, all right, and a wastebasket and a shared telephone and was allowed to use the company cafeteria. I knew nobody would probably ever read my name in the headlines on the business page, but I was a good, journeyman career-man and I worked every day.

It all comes to an end. You say it can't happen to you, but it happens. Your grip slips and you lose a major account in the woods. Your boss says to you, "I was expecting you to tee up that major account and knock it downtown for a hole-in-one that would have given us the go-ahead runs we needed in the late innings, but you lost it in the woods."

Concentration. I'd lost my concentration. And maybe my desire. It was when Lee Trevino and Pete Rose started to lose their concentration and their desire that they took little, bitty new wives. Now there's never a game where one of them isn't a contender. "You're off your game," my boss said. "You should do something before it's too late."

My wife had out her buck knife and was carving slices off a bar of soap into the Quaker Oats. She likes to serve oatmeal that has a nice, foamy head on it. I hesitated. I cleared my throat. Then I cleared the table. Then I cleared all my belongings out of the closets and cleared out of town.

That was no way to approach a subject that may have far-reaching effects on my career. I went back home.

"There are a lot of professional men," I said to my wife, "of which Lee Trevino and Pete Rose are two who spring to mind, who have done wonders for their careers late in the game by taking little, bitty new wives. I was wondering if there might not be something in their parallel stories that would provide a valuable lesson to us by way of career enhancement, not to mention brightening up the old place a bit?"

My wife looked up. "Were you talking to me?" she said.

TOMORROW: Will I pop the question? Tune in and hear me say, "Well, maybe I'll just get some new bags for the vacuum cleaner instead."

Talk it up

Infield chatter is the soul of banking. There were times in the banking game when we seemed to lack the winning spark. We would make bonehead transactions. Drop digits. Nothing would balance. Then one day the kindly old manager stuck his head out his office door and said, "Okay, let's talk it up out there. Let's hear a little chatter."

At first we found his suggestion embarrassing. We didn't exactly feel loose and comfortable with the idea of talking it up in the business-like surroundings of a bank. But the manager was a real team leader. "Cash that cheque, Joanie," he hollered. "Way to be, babe, way to be!" Our spirits rose. We knuckled down and felt tough and together. We felt like a team.

"How be, Joanie! Count them bills, babe. Make that change," we called encouragingly. Joanie squinted her eyes and hunched her shoulders. You could tell her concentration was getting sharper.

When somebody came in for a loan we'd look over toward the loans officer and call out, "Go for it, babe, go for it. Let's see that collateral, now. Lay it on the line." We became a bank to watch, and soon other institutions found our approach beneficial.

Not just financial institutions, either. Juries began to call encouragement to crooks. "Plead now, babe. Spit it on out. Spit it out there." And judges heartened witnesses who were on a hot streak: "Soundin' good, soundin' real good there."

Infield chatter does seem to help gather everybody's attention. Look what used to go on in operating rooms. Nurses would be yawning and thinking what they might have for lunch. The anaesthetist would be day-dreaming over his gauges. The surgeon would hold up one organ, then another, trying to recall what he was in there after. There was no cohesion, no sense of purpose.

But now – well, you can tell when, as they say, they've come to operate. "Gas him, babe. Gas him real good." And, "Way to cut, big cutter. Easy does it." And, "Get that appendix. That's it! Good eye, good eye." When patients learn how electrifying the atmosphere became while they were on the table they say they were sorry they had to sleep through it.

You don't see much bum-patting in the marketplace any more, though. It used to be Johnson would make a big sale – say Johnson was in the hosiery department and moved a tonne of Argyles – and the supervisor would acknowledge Johnson's achievement with a pat on the bum. Not any more.

Partly it's because of integration. Johnson as like as not is a woman these days and if she has too much success and gets too many pats the supervisor will find himself yanked in front of the Human Rights Commission for offering undue encouragement. Johnson will definitely get suspicious if she has a terrible day at the till, if she doesn't ring up a single sale, and as she is coming off the floor her supervisor says, "Great work, Johnson," and pats her bum.

Of course, there is always the possibility that Johnson is a homosexual. More and more of them are entering the business world. This led to a great deal of hesitancy when it came to bum-patting. Or, depending on the persuasion of the patter, to too much eagerness. One or the other.

Besides there's no telling what sex, if any, a supervisor might be any more. It all became terribly complicated. If bum-patting was going to persist, it would have had to develop a ritualized etiquette as complicated as anything ever found in an Imperial Japanese court.

That's why you see Supreme Court justices these days giving each other high-fives. One of them will write a particularly heady judgement and the brother and sister justices will all come racing together, their red robes flapping, and they'll leap into the air and smack each other on the open palm. "How to judge," they cry. "Hum-judge, hum-judge."

The high-five demonstrates undeniable exuberance, as well as involving contact only below the wrist, an area we have been taught since childhood was safe, insofar as any area of the anatomy is safe.

What we're doing in the bank now is getting a colour commentator to commentate on the action as it transpires during the day. Somebody like a Cosell or a Tony Kubek. It will add another dimension to the game. We've already got the TV cameras set up.

Icing the old folks

This is a real good time of year to watch the old folks slip and slide and fall down. The weather has been just about perfect for it.

The great thing is how convenient it is to watch. You don't have to line up for tickets and squeeze into some arena or theatre. You can just look out the window or keep an eye open when you go for a walk and you will hardly ever be disappointed.

When the old folks take a header it tends not to be too spectacular. That is because they can't travel very fast on sidewalks as tricky as these. Usually the old folks will be inching across an icy patch and – swoop! – out go the old feet and down comes the old body with a crunch on the hip or shoulder.

You hardly ever see old folks do an ankle-over-teacup loop or a full gainer. That doesn't mean it never happens. You just have to be lucky to spot one.

The snowplows provide nifty obstacles for old folks. At every intersection they block the sidewalk crossing with rugged little Alps that would have caused Hannibal to turn back in despair.

The old folks usually have trouble getting up the slippery grade and, often as not, topple over backward in the attempt. At the very least this knocks the wind out of them, but with a good enough whack it will dislocate something.

Should they make it to the top, there is a thrill a minute. The meltwater, that brown, briny gorp, accumulates in gulfs on the other side and the prospect of crashing on the perilous descent and pitching into that dreck often proves too much and the old folks simply lose heart. They collapse at the summit and roll to the bottom with a merry splash.

Private citizens have ample opportunity to bedevil old folks. There is an impression abroad that snowy sidewalks, if they are ever to be cleared, will be cleared by cherubim and seraphim dispatched by the Almighty when they have finished digging out His driveway.

By parking yourself in an easy chair in the window, you can watch old folks take spins and spills to your heart's content. It is considered unsporting to get out the garden hose and flood the sidewalk in front of your house, but some people are always more interested in quantity than quality and if you want to run up impressive numbers of old folks, it is a sure-fire way.

As far as I can see, if the old folks fall down a lot at this time of year, it is their own fault. It is because they have such brittle bones. You don't see young folks with brittle bones like that. Young folks are usually shrewd enough to have good resilient bones that are much harder to break and, when they break, mend in no time at all.

But old folks seem to favour brittle bones that snap like dry twigs and take forever to knit. When they walk out in the ice and snow, they walk as if they were carrying a big stack of fragile and expensive china – they walk very nervously, they are tense, they are scared.

This makes them easy marks. They are in the same bind as a batter in baseball who is fighting a slump. The more he worries about it, the more he tightens up and the more likely he is never to hit the ball. The old folks get themselves into a state and overcompensate and – swoop! – out go the old feet.

I recommend that the old folks get rid of those brittle bones and then just generally loosen up if they want to stop taking those nasty spills the rest of us get such a kick out of.

But – and when you face it, this is a compelling thought – why do they go out in the first place? They wouldn't be doing all this slipping and sliding, they wouldn't have trouble negotiating intersections, they wouldn't cry tears of frustration and rage because some fun-loving soul has left his sidewalk unshovelled, if they just stayed home.

Don't we have old folks' homes so the old folks can go there and stay out of harm's way? If they are going to insist on walking to the milk store or the mailbox, they're asking for trouble.

As I write this, more snow is falling. There is no need to worry that the old folks' follies will end for a while.

It is a pastime in which I am happy to be just a spectator. I wouldn't be one of the old folks if you paid me.

The skater

Donny Slattery was the only one at the pool party wearing skates. Everyone else was dressed for a hot, suburban Sunday afternoon – bathing suits, slacks, and loafers. Some of the women he had seen at home-and-school meetings wore light dresses with full skirts; some of the men he nodded to on the commuter train wore Madras sports jackets. There was grey in their hair, Donny Slattery saw. There was grey in his own.

People approached Slattery cautiously. They didn't appear to get the big laugh he expected they would at finding a cocktail guest dressed in a hockey uniform, a sweater that said "Bears," pants, stockings, skates, a helmet, and carrying a stick. Slattery asked the barman for another gin and tonic, a double.

"Where's Cheryl?" the woman who was head of the ratepayers' association asked.

"At the cottage with the kids." Slattery said.

The woman looked as if she was going to ask another question, but after a hesitation she shrugged and said, "I better dig up Phil. It's time we were on our way."

Slattery squirmed as sweat trickled down his back, between his shoulder pads. Cheryl and the kids had been away for a month when he discovered his old college duffel bag, with the whole kit inside, in the basement cold room. He didn't know he still had it. He'd been a tidy little defenceman in college, made intercollegiate all-star his last year, but "little" was the operative word and he'd given it up when he started to make a buck selling insurance. He was sure Cheryl had thrown the stuff out in one of their moves.

"You wearing a cup, too?" asked a man in polo shirt.

"You bet," said Slattery.

"Must be hot," said the man.

As the party broke up, Slattery narrowed his eyes and looked at the pool. He could imagine it frozen and smooth. He could imagine all the pools between here and the pool in his own backyard frozen and smooth. He wondered if he could skate all the way home.

There was a resounding splash. Women squealed as water spattered them. "Watch it!" they cried. Dumfounded, people looked into the pool and saw a hockey player in a gold and blue uniform, his heavy gloves flailing as he tried to stay afloat, fighting to gain the other side. He made it and hauled himself awkwardly out. "You okay, Donny?" someone called.

"Great," said Slattery, brandishing his stick in triumph. "Just great." He turned and climbed the fence into the next yard.

The patio around the next pool was empty. Slattery's skates left marks through the petunia bed and across a border of grass that looked as if someone had been chopping the earth with an axe. He cannonballed into the still, blue pool. A woman looked out a sliding glass door, saw the skater in her pool, and screamed.

He crossed yard after yard. "Mind if I skate across your pool?" Slattery asked. A man in a chef's hat tending a barbecue let a bottle of beer slip from his fingers. It smashed on the concrete. "What the – !" the man said. The splash made him duck.

Slattery was getting tired. His soaked uniform and the foam in the padding felt like it weighed 200 pounds. His heart boomed and his eyes clouded when he clambered out of the pools. Sometimes he slipped and fell back in two or three times.

"Not in as good shape as I used to be," he panted aloud to himself as he waded through a child's inflated pool, his skates slicing the plastic to ribbons. Terrified children scattered before him like leaves, wailing. "I used to be able to pick the puck up and go down the side as fast as Orr," Slattery said.

"As fast as Orr!" he hollered at the sobbing children.

He could hear the rising call of sirens approaching the neighbourhood. "I can outskate the cops!" he yelled at a pair of naked sunbathers who lay paralysed in fright as he heaved himself into their pool. "I used to be as fast as Orr!"

The sirens circled but never pinpointed his advance. It was night now, growing cool. Slattery shivered. He had no idea his house was so far away. The night grew darker. Lights went out.

At last he crashed into his own pool. It was empty. He struggled out and looked at his dark house. Windows were smashed, doors off their hinges. The furniture was gone. Dust and leaves littered the floors.

Slattery shivered. "These skates need to be sharpened," he said.

Bag-lady baseball

When the bag ladies play baseball, the announcer doesn't announce their lineup in the regular fashion: "Batting first and playing rightfield, so-and-so; batting second and playing third base, so-and-so; batting third and . . ." and so on, because the bag ladies don't go up to bat in any particular order and when they take the field they go and stand anywhere they please.

Sometimes, defensively, you might see three or four bag ladies in a sombre group between first and second base with their shopping bags in a circle around them. They might share wine from a bottle. The bag lady in rightfield has been known to spend the game staring away from the batter, over the rightfield fence, as if she were keeping watch for someone who was supposed to arrive from that direction.

When the bag lady who is catching lies down behind the plate and goes to sleep, the players on the other team keep their eyes averted and step around her warily. They pretend she isn't there. If there is a rain delay, the ground crew covers her with the field tarpaulin so she stays dry.

The bag ladies can't run very well; they can't even walk very well. They have knobbly old feet that pain them and when a bag lady draws a walk it takes forever for her to gather her shopping bags and get down to first base. Sometimes her feet hurt her so much – or something deep inside does, and she is afraid to imagine what it might be – that she will stop halfway and weep.

Every now and then when this happens the spectators along the first-base line will call a policeman to order the bag lady to move along. It spoils their day to have some filthy bag lady weeping in front of them; it spoils their view of the game. "Come on, dear," says the policeman. "Take your base or I'll have to take you in."

The bag ladies never swing at a pitch. Their eyes are blurry; a goodly number of them have cataracts. The only things they see clearly are things that might have happened in some time past to some pretty girl they might have been, but who knows? Bag ladies have notoriously faulty memories. They can't ever remember what the count is when they are at bat and sometimes they straggle back to the dugout after only one strike.

The bag ladies don't wear baseball uniforms. They wear their usual bag-lady get-ups, but these differ from individual to individual, as do the accessories. In general, they wear an overcoat over three or four cardigans and a dress that might have been brown. Not as many wear high-top running shoes as you think. It is as dangerous to stereotype a bag lady as anybody else.

Shabby oxfords with the heels worn flat are the most common footwear. Nobody knows where the shoes come from, just as nobody knows where the salmon spends the years and tides before it returns to its native stream. The origin of bag-lady shoes is one of the unsolved mysteries of nature.

The bag ladies' bags are filled with crumpled newspapers and children's clothes, actually infants' clothes, little tiny dresses and overalls and sleepers they have found in cans behind apartment buildings, although it is really none of our business. If a batter on the opposing team hits a ball that runs into a bag lady's bag and stops dead, it is a ground-rule double.

There was a big turnout to see the bag ladies play the Cincinnati Reds because everybody wanted to see Pete Rose. They wanted to see if Charlie Hustle still had his hustle. They wanted to see if he was still worth millions. They weren't disappointed. He knocked the first pitch into deep centre where it fell untouched. The crowd urged him to hit another and another, to keep going. Pete Rose showered the outfield with baseballs.

He filled the sky with a blizzard of baseballs. Soon the outfield was covered in white and balls began to pile up in drifts along the fence. The bag ladies made their uneasy way over the baseballs and huddled for protection in centrefield.

The storm was relentless. White drifts of baseballs swirled around the bag ladies and over them. When they disappeared from view the game was called and the Reds were declared winners. Pete Rose said he owed his success to hustle and more hustle.

Spitting it out

With the end of the baseball season, we come to the end of serious spitting on television. No other cultural entertainment, not hockey, not even opera, depends so much on spitting. Baseball is a game of ritual and spitting is as central to the ritual as the swinging censer is to the mass.

Nothing can be more edifying than to watch, in close-up, the sag-eyed Tom Lasorda leaning pale and reptilian in the corner of the Dodger dugout spt-spt-spitting a steady stream of tiny gobs so reminiscent of the flicking tongue of a marauding dragon.

Or to see Gary Carter, resplendent in the tools of his trade, turn sidewise from his ready posture behind the plate and raise the chin of his catcher's mask, a knight raising the visor of his helm, and unloose a fine brown jet behind the batter's knee. Battle is joined, he signifies, and the baseball juices are flowing.

Only baseball indulges so liberally in spit-enhancing chewing tobacco – by preference, shag-cut Red Man – to improve the quality of the product. Until you have strode across the artificial turf of Exhibition Stadium and felt your foot squish and lose, for a fraction of a second, traction on a slimy spot of big-league expectoration, you have not experienced the true richness and romance of the pastime.

No other sport names its most devastating weapon in honour of its guiding spirit: the spitball. The ball takes a sudden sharp swerve as it crosses the plate and everyone suspects slick treachery. There are a number of explanations why spit causes the ball to behave the way it does. None of them is sanitary.

My mother's late father liked baseball and adored Mickey Mantle. My mother's late father was a religious man, however, and would not spit on the Lord's Day. And he certainly never chewed tobacco. He was a religious man and spit naturally or not at all.

In my elementary school, spitting accuracy was much admired, especially if the spitter could spit between his teeth. Sometimes we played a game of spitting at one another and dodging. In these contests, horking was viewed dimly. A kid suspected of horking could end up with his face pushed in.

John Nance Garner, known as "Cactus Jack," was vice-president of the United States under Franklin Delano Roosevelt. Garner said, "The vice-presidency ain't worth a pitcher of warm spit."

I once worked on a farm with a man who kept a chaw in his right cheek. From the corner of his mouth, a dark drool of what looked like crankcase oil trickled constantly down a vertical wrinkle and formed a drop on his chin. Of all the things I ever had anything to do with on the farm, this gave me the most squeams.

Go ahead! Spit it out! – An encouragement to confess.

To spit in the River Liffey in Dublin is said to bring good luck. Travellers report that the Liffey stinks to high heaven.

Spit-in-the-ocean is a poker game in which each player is dealt four down cards and then one card is dealt face up in the middle to become the common wild card. Serious gamblers consider this game silly and refuse to play.

Guinness Book of Records: "In the 3rd International Spittin', Belchin', and Cussin' Triathlon, Harold Fielden reached 34 ft. ¼ in. at Central City, Colo., July 13, 1973. Distance is dependent on the quality of salivation, absence of cross wind, two-finger pucker and the co-ordination of the back arch and neck snap. Sprays or wads smaller than a dime are not measured."

The Leslie Street Spit, built entirely by man, extends into Lake Ontario for a distance of 3.2 miles and provides a nesting site for many birds.

The late Strother Martin, the actor who said, "What we have here is a failure to communicate," in *Cool Hand Luke*, spit dramatically in that film as well as in *The Wild Bunch* and *Butch Cassidy and the Sundance Kid*.

In the men's washrooms on Via Rail passenger coaches, a sign is posted advising that the fine for spitting is $40.

In any decent pool hall, the penalty for spitting is ejection.

This has been a particularly disgusting thing to write. I'm glad I don't have to read it.

Hat tricks

Of all the players on a baseball team, only the catcher wears his hat backwards. Of all the players on a baseball team, only the catcher faces out toward the field. This means that even though one player faces in a direction opposite the direction of the other players on his team, all their hats continue to point in the same direction.

This is an eternal verity of baseball and the only hat statistic that exists. This is a mystery itself in a game in which everything is enumerated, every imaginable element, down to the number of times a shortstop spit in his mitt, pounded it, and shouted "Hey, babe!" before making a catch off a left-handed hitter that started a double play.

In fact, it seemed strange that baseball players even wore hats, so stripped is the game of non-essential elements. Players spend little time in the sun, no more than half an inning at a time, and when it rains, they take shelter in the dugout. When they need protective headgear – when they're in the batter's box – they don it, often *over* their uniform hats.

(No other investigator has examined the undersides of the peaks of baseball hats. Many, it turns out, are painted in psychedelic designs with the initials of loved ones intricately worked into the motif. Some are decorated with hand-tinted photographs of shrines of favourite saints. Some have notices pinned to them advertising living-room suites for sale or dog-grooming services, with a fringe of phone numbers along the bottom that can easily be torn off.)

A student of the game will find it significant that while the baseball hat has very little apparent use while it is on the player's head, it assumes great value the instant it comes off, especially if that happens to be an instant when the player is tearing across the turf in pursuit of a long fly ball.

The flying-off-of-the-hat, as it is called in baseball parlance, shows the player is not nonchalanting. In baseball there is no sin greater than nonchalanting. When you nonchalant you beat yourself, as they say.

This need for the flying-off-of-the-hat would explain the aerodynamics of the hat's bill, shaped as it is like a sail that can catch the wind (taking inertia into account) as the player looks up for the baseball and sets off at a tremendous pace, causing the hat to fly off, dramatically.

I have made a survey of 317 outfield chances this season, of which 284 were successful. Of these 284, half the catches were made by players whose hats flew off, and half were made by players whose hats hadn't. There proved, thusly, to be absolutely no correlation between successful catches and the hattedness or non-hattedness of the fielder.

But – and here is the significant factor – in every instance where the player's hat flew off, it *looked* as if he was trying harder!

Which is the point worth understanding from this unfortunately somewhat academic consideration of the baseball hat, especially in light of all the drivel one hears about the applications of sporting contests to real life ("It matters not whether you win or lose," and other canards beyond number). Because this is the only instance where we really have something to learn.

These days it is difficult to work in an office and not appear to be nonchalanting. More and more of us work at video terminals and you tend to sit before them with the same open-mouthed, switches-off expression and the same what-the-hell posture as you do before the television at home.

Even though you might be run ragged by the computer, it is hard to look busy whilst being so run. So it becomes vital that when the boss calls, you appear to him keen, eager to do his (you know full well) dreary bidding. And there is no better way to demonstrate this than to have your hat fly off as you leave your desk and rush to his office.

Reward will come to you. Nary a suspicion of nonchalanting will cloud his brow. All you have to do is tie about three yards of fishing line to your hat and thumbtack the other end to the wall by your desk. When the call comes – zang! – your hat will spin in your wake.

It's what all the ballplayers do. The smart ones. The smart rich ones.

Baseball jargon

Enjoyment of baseball as a spectator sport, rather than as a diet supplement or a dance craze, is greatly increased by gaining some command of the jargon which infests the game as thickly as flies infest a manure pile on a glaring deep-summer day when there is no breeze and the smell doesn't drift away, when the smell shimmers in the heat and the buzz of flies, a sound as raw and shivery as a nail file being drawn over a sliver in your finger, is audible from 100 feet away in the humid stillness.

Knowledge of the jargon is easily acquired. Many acquire it by entering into a trance state and wafting moodily through the ectoplasm until they arrive at the cosmic essence of baseball, the yin and the yahoo of the game, which looks, they say, a lot like spit. Others pick it up in the street like it was some cheap tramp with too much rouge and too much mascara, a painted chippie with a lot of past and no history. Some have it surgically implanted.

Of course there are some people who say they don't want to know the jargon of baseball. They say the less they know about baseball the happier they'll be. They say baseball makes them throw up. Sick to their stomachs. To which we can only say, Well, you never know. What if there is a skill-testing question at the Pearly Gates? What if it has to do with baseball? Why put yourself out of the running by maintaining an aggressive ignorance of the game? That's what we say. Why not give yourself all the help you can?

If that makes good sense to you, please join with us now and garner a few bits of jargon from the prose offerings that follow, picking them as if they were ripened grapes crying out to be pressed into sweet wine, sweet wine sparkling with the mysterious music of dancing lights and feathery imaginings, sweet wine to be drunk by firm-fleshed maidens and mischievous youths edging impatiently forward in the springtime of desire.

– Imagine a baseball diamond, each base 90 feet from the next, the pitcher on the mound, 60 feet, 6 inches from home plate. The rest of the defensive nine is arrayed on the field defensively. On the bases, the first two at any rate, stand runners and at the plate stands a batter. If the batter hits a home run, that is, if he strikes the baseball thrown by the pitcher with such force that it goes out of the park, scoring three runs – himself and the two runners already on base – the team at bat will win. If he fails to do so, the team in the field will win.

The pitcher pitches, the batter hits the ball. It loops into the outfield and the centrefielder catches it on the first bounce. When he catches the ball, the centrefielder whirls and throws it as hard as he can over the wall and into the farthest row of the stands. This lets the three runs, including the winner, score.

What is the appropriate baseball jargon for this play by the centre-fielder? It is called "*an extremely odd thing to do*."

– Imagine the same baseball diamond. A scoreless game, two out, the bottom half of the third inning. The shortstop calls time and trots off the field. He reappears in a few minutes driving a bulldozer and followed by two trucks carrying workmen and building materials. He bulldozes a clear, level patch around his fielding position and the workmen, who waste no time, erect a variety store, a donut shop, a dry cleaners, and a hardware store, which includes a post office, in a tidy row. While they do this, the shortstop paves the infield and paints a grid of white lines on it to indicate parking spaces.

What is this play by the shortstop called in the jargon of baseball? It is called "*building a plaza between second and third*."

– Imagine the same baseball diamond, only this time several more bases have been added at random. The pitcher is bashful and refuses to throw to the batter, so the second baseman is pitching from second base. He throws a fastball inside which the batter hits straight up. The ball goes up and up and up. It disappears from sight. It never comes down. Nobody can look anybody else in the eye.

The baseball jargon for this is "*strange goings on*." It is marked in the scorebook thusly: SG.

Hawks, a golden eagle, a golden afternoon

The wind is out of the north-northeast and the hawks are riding it. After winter's purge, the land begins slowly to fill up again. It is a tidal rhythm and now the hawks flow with it through the wilderness of sky. The migration of birds is one of the world's great mysteries, one that man with his charts and laboratories and studies and com-

puters is still a good distance away from unravelling. We know most of the whats; we can plot them on graphs; but most of the hows remain little more than surmise.

The migration is a mystery in much the same way that beauty is a mystery, and if we hold that there is any value in such commodities as poetry and love and wonder, it is a good thing that this is so. The migration will probably remain a mystery as long as there is anything about life that we consider miraculous.

The late Brooks Atkinson, who was best known as a theatre critic, kept an eye on the sky as well and came as close as anybody to explaining what we ought to see in the northward flight of the hawks. "Although birds co-exist with us on this eroded planet," he wrote, "they live independently of us with a self-sufficiency that is almost a rebuke. In the world of birds a symposium on the purpose of life would be inconceivable. They do not need it. We are not that self-reliant. We are the ones who have lost our way."

A low-pressure system has moved below the Great Lakes from the west. In a day or two its easterly winds should bring rain, but until then the hawks course along on these winds, wings spread, as if they were surfing on a vast, invisible wave. Most of them in our part of the world glide up the Niagara Peninsula, buoyed on the air masses that billow up from the cliffs and thawing heights of the escarpment. The escarpment is the hawks' spring expressway.

The hawk watchers gather atop it in a ragged clearing in the Beamer Memorial Conservation Area. Through the trees to the north and a long way straight down lie Grimsby and the Queen Elizabeth Way, through the trees to the east 40-Mile Creek crashes down a limestone canyon, bound for Lake Ontario. The lake spreads away through the green-blue spectrum to the dark deeps at the horizon. This is the tenth year there has been an organized watch here during the hawk migration, which runs from the tag-end of February through May, ten years of dressing mystery in columns of figures. For the record, as many as 16,300 have been counted in a single spring.

Today promises good numbers and the birds are travelling low enough that a novice watcher almost gets the feeling he can tell one species from another. The hawk-eyed veterans of the count can see a bird that is little more than a pinprick, even when magnified by binoculars, and in an instant tell the species, age, sex, what it had for breakfast, and how it is likely to vote.

At times there are a dozen birds above at once and the watchers call them off in a shorthand: "Tail," "Shoulder," "Sharpie," "T.V." for red-tailed, red-shouldered, sharp-shinned – all hawks; T.V. is the turkey vulture teetering across the sky on forbidding black wings.

Most of the birds pass overhead in a flash and the voices raised in shouts of identification, and laughing dispute, and efforts to keep the tally straight, make a carnival noise. This is live action and exciting. "They're pouring in!" someone shouts. "They're pouring in!" Today, when the count winds up at four p.m., 617 will have poured in.

That the hawks are predators and are fierce adds an extra measure to their self-reliance. They are hunters, and small creatures move warily when the hawks are flying. Each is designed as a nearly perfect instrument, one that is guided by instinct in the terrible and bloody and glorious business of staying alive.

And none is so glorious as this huge black bird that sails above the treetops in the minutes shortly past noon: a golden eagle, the sun glancing off its irridescent head as if from a mirror-bright helmet. A tumult of cheers erupts from the watchers. The passage of the eagle is a rare and special sight. For a moment we are small creatures. For a moment in that clearing man's position in the scheme of things is stood on its head.

There's something about an eagle that puts things in perspective.

5

Painless Politics

Options

The prime minister took a sheet of paper and at the top of it wrote, "Don't vote for the Tories or they are going to send you back to Italy." It was a quote from his finance minister, who claimed this was the sort of thing the Liberals had been saying during the election campaign.

Then the prime minister began examining his options. He had to do this every time the finance minister said something. It kept him hopping.

He wrote, "Option A. Deny whole thing categorically." That was usually the safest thing to do when his finance minister said something, but maybe not this time. His party had, after all, just won a mighty victory. What if they had won it because the Liberals had been saying the Tories would send everybody back to Italy?"

That would mean he was elected because everybody expected him to send them back to Italy. They took it as a tacit promise. And the prime minister was determined to live up to his promises, tacit or not. He wrote, "Option B. Send everybody back to Italy." That would get him off the hook.

Then again, it might not. Especially if it was true that the Liberals had lost all credibility and nobody believed them when they said the Tories would send everybody back to Italy. If he sent everybody back to Italy he would restore Liberal credibility while severely damaging his own.

In that case, "Option C. Send only those people back to Italy who came from there." Who could complain about that? Except the only people who came from Italy were Italians. If he appeared to be favouring one group over another there would be an uproar. If people thought he was less than even-handed it could hurt his chances next election.

"Option D" became clear. "Send everybody back to Italy except the Italians. Send the Italians someplace else." But the transportation costs would be astronomical. And who would pay for it? All the taxpayers would have been sent back somewhere. Increasing costs while decreasing the revenue base was the sort of financing he had pledged to stop.

Drastic measures were called for. "Option E. Take everybody's money and then send them back." Here was an idea he could support. It was along the lines of how he'd put the kibosh on criticism that he was opposed to universality with the baby bonus. Why, universality was sacred to him. Absolutely sacred. So he abided by the law that said every man-jack was entitled to get it. Then, he passed a law saying everybody wasn't entitled to keep it. And he took it back.

Neat. But when he thought about it, the places he was sending everybody back to wouldn't let in a bunch of penniless immigrants. They'd all be deported back to Canada where they'd be just as penniless. Then he'd have to put the entire population on welfare. That would look bad, him being a Conservative and all.

"Option F. Find more options." Quickly. "Option G. Claim that what the finance minister said had been misconstrued." Trouble was every time his ministers said something awkward, somebody tape-recorded it. If somebody else didn't tape-record it, the ministers tape-recorded it themselves and sent it out to radio stations.

"Option H. Okay, so he said it. But it was in a weak moment of camaraderie with a reporter and, Lord knows, I've had a few myself." He liked that. The old it-could-happen-to-anybody-even-me. Except it wasn't supposed to. After it had happened to him he had expressly ordered members of his government not to have weak moments of camaraderie with reporters. Or any moments, for that matter. So was he the leader or wasn't he? None of his ministers would dare go against a direct order.

In which case, "Option I. Explain that whoever made the statement couldn't have been the finance minister. It had to be an imposter." Everybody would sympathize with the prime minister because an imposter was going around saying things that got the prime minister in hot water. He wouldn't mind getting that sympathy vote.

And when the imposter brought down a budget in a few months' time, the prime minister would be free to deny the whole thing.

Judging by the way things were going he might want to. It was an option worth keeping open.

Open to hostilities

It was disappointing to hear Prime Minister Brian Mulroney turning weak and snivelling about accepting the generous offer of the United States to let us join the research on the "Star Wars" scheme to create a space-based anti-missile system.

Especially after Joe Clark, the external affairs minister, and a man who has his head screwed on tight, pointed out that we stood to gain some jobs from the $26 million venture.

These jobs would help bridge the gap between the present period of high unemployment and the period of total unemployment that would follow the deployment and use of the system in a global conflict.

The gang here at the Strategic Initiatives Research Centre was depressed as anything by these developments, but we perked up when the prime minister went on to say he wasn't all that crazy about participating in anything "where you're not a big player, where you don't set the thrust and where you have no control over the parameters," because that reminded us of something we've been noodling around with on the computer that might just be the ticket.

And it would sure make the external affairs minister happy because, as we like to say, there's nothing like a good little war to put the country to work. That's what we call this initiative: A Good Little War.

It's not all worked out yet, but the gist is that to be a big player, all we have to do is pick somebody and declare war on them. We probably shouldn't pick somebody we don't like, since this isn't one of those negative wars of aggression that are public relations nightmares. Besides, most of the countries we don't like could wipe us off the map in about twenty seconds.

We should pick a country we don't care about in the least. And it should be one that's an even match for us in terms of military might, since we'll want this war to go on for some time. It's no good to fill people's pockets and create an atmosphere of rising expectations and then have the whole thing suddenly end because one side or the other wins. We'd end up in the same boat as before.

We're nominating Ecuador. Not one Canadian in 10,000 can dredge up the slightest feeling one way or the other about Ecuador, or locate it on a map. As for the Ecuadorian military forces, who knows? – which is precisely what international defence analysts say when they assess Canadian military forces.

As for thrust, the prime minister can choose any thrust he likes. He could fly our army off to invade them, but when you do that you're playing on the other guy's parameters, and who knows if we could even find the place? A better thrust would be to have them invade us. That way we'd have home-parameter advantage and, while we want to be fair about this, a little edge never hurt anybody.

Since we don't know what might prompt Ecuador to open hostilities against Canada, the gang here at the Strategic Initiatives Research Centre has been studying the problem, and we believe the most effective method would be taunts. We put up billboards and buy some radio and TV spots that say, "Ecuador, you stink!" and "You're a dope, Ecuador," and "Ecuador can't lick its own lips." Then we sit back and wait.

NEWSFLASH: Ecuador invades Canada. A powerful Ecuadorian force thought to number in the twenties has landed on the Leslie Street Spit and begun a steady advance behind a line of armored llamas.

As soon as the Canadian army got back from lunch it could be mobilized in the station wagon and driven down to the front to mount a stalwart defence. It would be nice for our boys, because they would live close to their war. "Hi, honey, I'm home." "How goes the battle, dear? Now don't just throw that dirty old gun there. Put it in the closet where it belongs."

Munitions plants will be crying for workers, as will allied industries such as the service station where the station wagon is gassed up and repaired. Hotels will fill with war correspondents who will rush from bar to bar, drinking up their expense accounts.

Sadly, there will be casualties. Somebody will get stepped on by a llama or get shot dead. But these are the perils of any war, and every man who falls means a job opening in the line for a brave, new soldier.

Playing for laughs

Mila Mulroney and Geills Turner are a couple of great gals and through all the backing and forthing between them over Stornoway, the Opposition Leader's official residence, I have been wondering something.

I have been wondering why I don't write a humorous column about their wrangle. It seems to cry out for something stinging by way of satire.

But say I was to take a crack at it, what would I write? I mean, what could I write that could possibly be any sillier than the simple facts of the case? The phantom furniture, the kitchen with no drawers, the shrill vituperation, the panic to spend taxpayers' money so it won't lie around and go bad.

Say you were a satirist and your job depended on you satirizing two of history's great strutters and posers, two men so dazzled by their own awesome importance that they have to wear sunglasses when they shave, and say you dreamed up a story about how the country they were supposed to run got put on hold while their wives conducted a vendetta over renovations and furniture.

Well, forget it. You'd be out of work. It would be too far-fetched. Satire has to have at least a whiff of plausibility and nobody would buy that nonsense.

The Stornoway episode is another dismal demonstration of the death of satire. Satire looks as if it is going to stay dead until our leaders stop being ridiculous. Right now they're so ridiculous that the most lunatic thing a satirist can imagine them saying or doing is nowhere near as lunatic as what they actually *will* say and do.

Word of satire's death came with Watergate. A couple of years earlier, Philip Roth wrote *Our Gang*, a novel about the brigands in the Nixon White House. Roth had Nixon bugging his own conversations. He had Nixon and his cabinet dressed in football uniforms and helmets as they gathered for pre-game prayers in the bunker. He had them utter operational truths.

Then along came that slapstick burglary and the Cubans and Martha Mitchell and Spiro Agnew and "I am not a crook," and by the time Nixon stepped into the helicopter and ascended from the White House lawn, one thing was clear: Roth at his most hysterical, Roth in his wildest imaginings, never imagined anything as sensationally ridiculous as what actually happened. Instead of appearing prescient, Roth appeared to suffer from puniness of vision.

If a satirist had set out to do a wicked number on Pierre Trudeau, a man whose sad destiny it was to lead a country smaller than his ego, he might picture the great democrat and intellectual, with the last prime ministerial flourish of his pen, giving kissy-face jobs to every Liberal who ever sent him a Christmas card. But no satirist on earth would have had the moxie to suggest Bryce Mackasey be appointed ambassador to Portugal. And no satirist would ever go so far as to present John Turner as the patsy in these shenanigans.

Okay, so Trudeau shoved another knife into satire's lifeless back. Did B. Mulroney leave the corpse lying there? No, first he rose to the tip of his tippy-toes in indignation about Trudeau's patronage – but that was fairly predictable. Then he feinted a bit and deked a bit. And then in one magnificent swoop he booted every Liberal off the Air Canada board and stacked it with the glory of Tory hackdom, the lame and the halt and the former mayor of York.

There never was a satirist with a brush as sweeping as that, or one who would have iced the cake by offering a Senate appointment to the former editor-in-chief of *The Globe and Mail*, the man who had been the most outspoken foe of the Senate and patronage in the nation. And it's certain no satirist would have been so shameless as to have the former editor-in-chief *accept* the appointment.

With Mulroney driving his bulldozer over the broken form of satire, would any satirist dream of illustrating the rebirth of reaction in the United States by having President Reagan receive invitations to visit an SS cemetery and an extermination camp in West Germany, and have him turn down the camp in favour of the Nazi cemetery?

Of course not, because a satirist firmly believes there are limits to everything, even the ridiculous.

Shadow of the cruise

Look at the faces of children for some mark, some sign. The children are the first generation born to a world where men possess the astonishing power to kill all of them – all of the children everywhere – in an instant, blinding and final. You'd think there would be something in their faces to indicate they had been born into a time as terrible as that.

Every generation until now, mine, my father's, his father's, on back to Noah's and the generations that begat him and that begat them before him, has considered the idea that the world might end. Some people have made reputations for themselves predicting just when it would happen. Some of us have always thought this to be worthwhile information, giving us a chance to put on clean underwear and pay the Hydro and make peace with our God or gods.

But that has always been pure speculation, and would continue to be if the world were left to its own devices. If it were, you would find nothing in the faces of children today that you couldn't have found in the faces of children down the long ages preceding them.

Now the date of the end is no longer purely speculative. Now it can be arrived at by committee decision, by presidential choice, by accident, by miscalculation, by blood spilled out among the stars.

The children walking past my window on the way to school were born in a time when there are men in the world who, if they want to, can take a pencil and draw a circle around a date on the calendar and say that day will be the end of time. The end of time for all time. And it will be. This is a different proposition entirely and if I were a child today I would not be happy about it.

Those of us of earlier generations have lived, however briefly, in a hopeful time, a time when it was impossible, except for mystics, to speak so positively about the end of things. The world blundered along, bumbled along. Sometimes the horsemen broke out. War, pestilence, famine, death, they galloped back and forth across the landscape, laying waste. But they could always be called back – at least to some extent; could be contained – at least to some extent; apart from death, of course, but all things being equal and with a fair wind and a bit of luck, death usually didn't show up until his appointed time.

If you looked in the faces of the generations before this latest one – before the generation born to the realization that it might be the last one – I think you might see a mark: a faint cast of innocence, perhaps, because we once, however briefly, lived in a world where hope for all mankind was not hostage to the demonic technologies within the reach of a few powerful, political men.

I stop by the rink in the park and watch children from what could be the last generation rush end to end, hollering after the puck. Does the ice feel different under their skates? Does the sight of their shadows chasing them, matching them stride for stride, offer up some image only they can see? "Pass it! Pass it! Over here!" Many voices. Does the outcome of this pickup game in the February sun matter in ways that games never mattered before?

Does a cheeseburger taste different to them? A chocolate milkshake? How about French fries with gravy, knowing that on some strategic planner's plotting table is a model based on calculations that this cheeseburger and this chocolate milkshake and these French fries will be the last ever? These are questions that can't be answered because to these children in this hangout after school this is the way these things have always tasted. It is all they know.

And love. I'm not sure that I know all that much about how love feels (although there are moments when I think I know quite a bit about it), but then I am inclined to think finding out might take forever and then some. What of these children who are falling in love today? Do they see love as a commodity that must be divvied up and consumed before it is too late? Can they hear a meter running? When they walk by my window holding hands does it feel different than when I walked down a street holding hands with my first girl?

Yesterday the cruise missile flew again. Nothing like that happens in isolation. I believe I saw the shadow of the missile cross the faces of the children heading home, holding hands.

Following the leader

"The recurrent political phenomenon that he who seems to win loses and vice-versa appears to have little applicability in the recent Canadian and U.S. elections." These words were written by Conrad Black, the megalomillionaire journalist, and no one on earth had the foggiest idea what they meant except Brian Mulroney, the recently elected Canadian prime minister, to whom they were all too applicable. Tragically applicable. This is his story.

Brian Mulroney had not wanted to be prime minister. When he was just a little lad in Baie Comeau he had been asked what he wanted to be when he grew up and had answered, "Anything but prime minister." But he fell in with the wrong crowd and, as so often happens, the prime ministership was forced upon him.

At first he tried to hide the fact. Whenever the television cameras were turned on him he would announce the temperatures in Medicine Hat and Trois Rivières and describe a cold front that was headed this way from Michigan. He hoped people would think he was the weatherman on the local news. That's what he had really wanted to be. That's why he'd had a voice job.

A weatherman with Mulroney's natural-born falsetto would have no credibility. Viewers wanted a weatherman with a voice that rumbled like bowling balls inside a bass drum. Then when they heard a cold front was headed their way from Michigan, they knew they were in for it. So he'd had his voice changed surgically.

But people soon caught on, and he had no choice but to take the reins of the ship of state and try to keep it from plunging farther down the slippery slope.

Brian Mulroney decided the best thing a prime minister could do was set a good example for the rest of the country. If the prime minister was disorganized and iffy and showed up for work late, it was small wonder the country was disorganized and iffy and late for work. If the prime minister used a new broom and was careful with a dollar, the country would do the same, providing it could get its hands on a dollar to be careful with.

He began with a bold stroke. He shuffled his family. He told his daughter Caroline that she had been a daughter for eight years and was getting set in her ways. He wanted fresh blood in the daughter's position and was promoting his five-year-old son Mark to take her place. Caroline could take over as Mark. She would bring a female point of view to the traditionally male role of youngest son and find out whether she had what it took to make it in a boy's world.

Ben, the ten-year-old, took being the eldest son for granted. Ben was sent packing. To replace him, Mulroney brought in Sacha Trudeau from Montreal. To critics who complained that Sacha was an unhappy reminder of the previous government, the prime minister replied that it was important in a prime minister's family to have people with experience.

Sacha had almost a lifetime of experience. His appointment also proved the prime minister wasn't above crossing party lines to get the children he wanted. No one could accuse him of patronage.

Things were working out nicely for the prime minister until he was reminded of his sacred campaign promise that his children's nanny would not be on the public payroll. This would be small comfort in a country where most children didn't have nannies, much less daddies who controlled the public payroll. A grand gesture was called for.

The only equitable thing would be not to have his children on the public payroll, either. Who could complain of being fired from the public service when the fat was being trimmed from the prime minister's own family? He called his daughter Mark and his son Caroline and little Sacha in one at a time and told them they were being let go. "Clear out your toy chests," he said.

But in this winter of hard times it was winter and times were hard. There was no work for little children. A prime minister can know no disgrace greater than to have his former loved ones collecting unemployment insurance. A prime minister can know nothing lonelier than the long corridors of 24 Sussex empty of children's laughter.

"Winners, weepers," said Brian Mulroney, and bowed his head.

Feeling at home

Once upon a time, not so long ago, as a diplomatic courtesy, William Davis, the premier of Ontario, permitted our bars to remain open an extra two hours so the delegates to an International Monetary Fund conference wouldn't get the impression that people in Ontario live under some kind of repressive regime.

He also sold the world bankers tax-free booze so that after a hard day of staving off intergalactic economic collapse they could drink themselves comatose without suffering the personal economic collapse the good citizens of Ontario suffer when they try to do the same.

He explained he was doing this because some of the Moolah Moguls came from countries where the laws are different and he wanted them to feel at home. That is to say, when in Toronto the Romans would still prefer to do as the Romans do.

Some of the natives were upset about this. What the devil, they said. Here is Bill Davis, that paragon of rectitude, or words not even vaguely to that effect, saying there will be two laws in his domain, one for the rich and powerful and one for the rest of us. He must think we are chopped liver.

Pas du tout. Not at all. Bill Davis was just a terrific host and was probably disappointed that there wasn't time to do more to show that our humble province is the equal of the great countries from which the financial wizards had come.

It's too bad he didn't get a chance to legalize prostitution for the week they were here. A lot of those countries have state-run whorehouses and the premier, doubtless, had he thought of it, would have reserved a hotel and filled the rooms with shady ladies who could make sure the delegates didn't want for affection.

And think of the chance he missed to waive the laws on pornography. How much more comfortable some of our visitors would have been to find a stack of hard-core publications beside the Gideons in their bureaus. Some of them, perhaps, were accustomed to making their own, so it's a shame they couldn't phone room service and order up a couple of speed freaks and a Polaroid to ease the burdens of their deliberations. Surely the Humane Society would have been eager to go along and not protest when a Doberman pinscher was enlisted in the cause.

But these are mere delights of the flesh, recreational pastimes some delegates had long been accustomed to in their home countries. We wanted them to feel that Toronto does more than emulate them in the realms of good times.

For instance, in some of their countries it is considered bad form for women to walk around with their faces uncovered; in some places, indeed, it is an offence. A good host, as Bill Davis was certainly striving to be, would have gone a long mile in this direction and arranged to have women publicly flogged for not wearing veils.

That would have been a nice touch at a flashy reception on the lawn at Queen's Park. Between sips of Ontario champagne and mouthfuls of fried shrimp, the premier could have called his wife to the platform, introduced her, condemned her, and then beaten her within an inch of her life. "We couldn't have done it better ourselves," some delegates would have said.

I'm positive some of the delegates were homesick because none of us natives were visited at three a.m. by masked men and taken outside and summarily machine-gunned or, failing that, at least taken into the basement at police headquarters to have electrodes affixed to our genitals. Polite society isn't polite society in a lot of countries our visitors hailed from unless there are screams in the background.

If he had it to do all over again, Bill Davis would have been able to declare martial law and suspend the democratic process while the great conference was in session. I'm sure many of our guests were nervous to think that the streets were full of voters.

And this that you're reading. Something like this might have ruined some delegates' stay in our city. This wouldn't have been allowed where they came from. A good host would have taken over the press.

Me, I broke all my fingers. It was my way of saying "Welcome!"

Politics makes strange dead fellows

Here is a recent entry in the log of telephone calls received by *The Star*'s city desk: "1:10 p.m. Caller says she doesn't know whether her MP is alive or dead."

There is no hint of how the caller felt about this lack of knowledge. Relieved? Perhaps she was calling to register a sigh of relief. She had been annoyed with her MP for years. He was always underfoot when she tried to vacuum; he was always banging on the door just when she climbed into the tub; he was always providing her with public works projects – a new post office or an airport – when all she wanted was peace and quiet. But then he'd stopped coming around. Maybe he got the message. And now, Whoopee! (I'm paraphrasing) she doesn't know whether he is alive or dead.

It could be that. It seems more likely she was filing a complaint. "He came on like a demon lover, all hot and full of promise when he wanted my vote. But, now he's elected, my calls aren't returned, my billets doux come back unopened, I can't get a new post office or an airport for love nor money. I honestly don't know whether he's alive or dead."

It occurred to me these were glib interpretations based on an assumption that the caller was passing comment on being ignored by her MP when it could be she was not at all. It could be she was describing a problem literally. It could be her MP had paid her a pastoral visit and while she was pouring him a cup of tea she realized she couldn't tell whether he was alive or dead.

Or maybe she had seen him at a local function. MPs are regularly invited to grace a sod-turning or a first communion or a taffy pull and are called on to say a few words. The average MP, up on his hind legs in front of an audience, can give a fairly strong impression that he has been listed among the deceased.

It can be awkward at times. There's nothing an MP enjoys more than a chance to drop by a funeral parlor to pay his respects. There's something about a funeral parlor that makes an MP feel right at home. But often when he tries to leave the MP will be flattened by the undertaker who, acting under the mistaken impression that the departing MP was a client attempting to escape, nails him with a flying tackle. When even professionals can be so easily fooled, what hope have mere constituents?

That's what the caller must have been getting at. Her MP could be alive; he could be deader than yesterday's news. What she wanted to know was how to tell the difference.

Well, it's not easy. It has been made more difficult in recent years by the parties' practice of filling out their slates of candidates by taking names off tombstones and putting them on the ballots. (Usually it's the only way they can get candidates who aren't lawyers. With lawyers it doesn't much matter one way or the other.) The more of these candidates the party has that get elected, the more it can demonstrate that much-admired characteristic: party unity.

Very rarely a live one slips through and offers something perky from the backbench. Any sign of life on the backbench is construed as disloyalty. A live backbencher is called a "maverick." Occasionally a maverick will cross the floor and be elevated to the cabinet and breathe his last. The cabinet is known as "the Great Reward."

For MPs on the government benches the appeal of going to "the Great Reward" is so powerful that ambitious candidates who have sought to achieve it have had themselves freeze-dried in order to pass as dead. This can be risky. In the bright heat of TV lights a cabinet minister will sometimes begin to thaw and make unfortunate statements.

The matter is complicated even more by our devotion to Canada's state religion, a religion that holds Ottawa to be Heaven, as in the frequently expressed sentiments of newly elected MPs who realize that if they can keep their mouths shut for a few years they will be eligible for an indexed pension: "I think I've died and gone to Heaven."

(If it turns out that Ottawa really is Heaven, a lot of us are going to be keenly disappointed.)

I called Ottawa and asked how we could tell if our MPs were alive or dead. Ottawa told me the information was classified.

To thine own self be false

When Jim Coutts, the oldest established permanent floating Liberal candidate in town, sought the advice of the departing Prime Minister, Pierre Trudeau, on whether he should stand for the leadership of the party, Trudeau advised him to "Use your head and use your guts and make up your own mind."

Gosh. Listen, I consider myself a connoisseur of advice, maybe because I get so much of it. The first words my father spoke to me were, "Keep your nose clean." And I personally wouldn't give Trudeau a wooden nickel for the advice he gave Coutts. Only somebody accustomed to dispensing Liberal nostrums could come up with something as mugwumpish as that.

Although Coutts called it "sound advice," it is in fact non-advice, and while there is a time and a place for non-advice, Trudeau's offering ranks with the pompous dodderings of dribbly old Polonius advising his dim-witted son. "To thine own self be true."

Imagine it: I think I'm going to kill myself. "Use your head and use your guts and make up your own mind." "To thine own self be true." Thanks, guys.

It's the kind of advice you get from somebody who wants to, or ought to, mind his own business. A person seeking advice wants something *useful*, although you should bear in mind that Lord Chesterfield, who gave his son more advice than he could carry in a wheelbarrow, said, "Advice is seldom welcome; and those who want it most always like it the least."

Here's some twenty-four-carat Chesterfield advice: "Women who are indisputably beautiful or indisputably ugly are best flattered upon the score of their understandings; but those who are in a state of mediocrity are best flattered upon their beauty, or at least their graces; for every woman who is not absolutely ugly thinks herself handsome."

Advice doesn't always have to be so wordy. "Run to daylight!" was Vince Lombardi's advice in the backfield as in life. St. Paul, never one to keep his own counsel, tersely advised the folks in Corinth that "It is better to marry than to burn." But Paul had the sort of robust background that stands an advice-giver in good stead. I swear by his advice to Timothy: "Drink no longer water but use a little wine for thy stomach's sake."

Among the most sensible words ever spoken were Roy Blount Jr.'s advice on hats. "Don't wear a Greek fisherman's hat unless you are a) Greek and b) a fisherman." Further on hats, heed the anonymous adviser who said, "Never wear a hat that has more character than you do." Then, considering the whole wardrobe, who can argue with Thoreau's advice that we "Beware of all enterprise that requires new clothes."

Advice can be cruel. Machiavelli advised the Prince that "Whoever desires to found a state and give it laws must start with assuming that all men are bad and ever ready to display their vicious nature, whenever they may find occasion for it." Perhaps it was that sort of advice that prompted Hermann Goering to come up with some of his own. "Shoot first and inquire afterwards," he said.

But even bad guys can deliver the goods. When Eli Wallach, the villain in *The Good, The Bad and The Ugly*, was luxuriating in a bubble bath he was surprised by an enemy who, gun drawn, gave a long speech about why he was going to kill Wallach. There was a sudden explosion of bubble bath – Wallach had his own gun hidden in the tub – and the enemy fell down dead. Wallach advised the departed, "If you're going to talk, talk. If you're going to shoot, shoot."

And you can't have a worthwhile discussion of advice without including what some consider the greatest advice ever given. It was given by the novelist Nelson Algren. "Never play cards with a man called Doc. Never eat at a restaurant called Mom's. And never, ever, no matter what you do in the rest of your life, never go to bed with a woman who has more problems than you."

It is in that tricky area between men and women that one gives advice at one's peril. That's where non-advice such as Trudeau gave Coutts is safest. A lover never gives an adviser credit, but an adviser always gets the blame. So from now on I'll say, "Use your head and use your guts and make up your own mind." Then I'll light a candle to Ann Landers.

As the Crow passes

For the last while we have been trying to learn to live without the Crow's Nest Pass freight rate. It has not been an easy time.

We have found ourselves looking up from our homely tasks and staring off into space for hours on end, our brains idling rhythmically, *half a cent a ton-mile, half a cent a ton-mile*. Great is our loss. Our loss inhabits every recess of our beings.

Not that we used the Crow ourselves. We never had any grain to ship from Prairie elevators to West Coast terminals. Not a bushel, not a peck. It wasn't our thing.

Our thing was spiritual. It was the spirituality of the Crow's Nest Pass freight rate that spoke to us, that spoke to us in a language beyond words, that said things words cannot convey nor thoughts comprehend. Perhaps the heart's embrace alone could grasp the message. Perhaps not. We don't know. It never made any sense to us at all. That is the way of spiritual things.

The Crow's Nest Pass freight rate has been with us from the beginning. It may have been with us from before the beginning, but we don't know. We don't go back that far. We only go back to the beginning. That's where we got our start.

Mothers cradled us in their arms, crooning the Crow's Nest Lullaby. *Half a cent a ton-mile.* Fathers taught us the facts of life. *Half a cent a ton-mile.* Teachers drilled us. Preachers wrote it with lightning bolts on the tender tabulae rasae of our eternal souls. Dirty old persons waylaid us in unsavoury beverage rooms and poured the resonant formula into our shell-like ears. *Half a cent a ton-mile.* And we got the message.

It was embedded in our beds, ingrained in our grain, and if you look into the interstices of our lives, you will find it is what they are full of, the way that part of the chesterfield behind the cushions is full of change and bits of cookies and ratty grey Kleenexes and the tops off ballpoint pens and round brown things that might be Glossette Raisins and unidentified grit in general.

In the warp and woof of daily experience, the Crow's Nest Pass freight rate was the warp, or the woof, depending on your point of view, with a 4 per cent margin for error either way seventeen times out of twenty or thereabouts. In the world of baggy-pants philosophers, it was what held our trousers up. In the naughty limerick of life, it's what gave our vice its versa, and, for all we know, put the ram in the ramma-damma-ding-dong.

Without it the sunset will not be a glorious blaze of colours in the western sky, but just one more light going out. Chopin will not be a charm to still the savage breast, but a noisy party in the next apartment and its three in the morning and you have to get up for work soon. Food will lose its flavour. Booze will lose its bang.

Love will no longer be loving, it will just be a cheap physical thing. With the willowy brunette who wears the green leotard in aerobics class, with any luck. Maybe in some motel on the lakeshore. Maybe the one that has the waterbeds. See? See how absolutely squalid life becomes, now the Crow is gone?

We meet in nervous groups, pale outlines of the shadows of our former selves. "Me and the old lady, we don't have nothing in common any more," one of us says, voice choked, hesitant.

"Have you tried the General Agreement on Tariffs and Trade?"

"Yeah. It wasn't the same."

"How about the Auto Pact? The Auto Pact is still in effect, isn't it?"

"You'd think there'd be nothing wrong with a little Crow's Nest Pass for old time's sake. But nope. There's nothing there."

"*Half a cent a ton-mile*," we said. "*Half a cent a ton-mile*." In unison. A tremulous chorus that rose, and then fell, and then died. The words turned to ashes. Our hearts turned to stone.

One by one we rose and slipped away into the eyeless night. For some, money is god, for some, power. They're the smart ones. We wanted the Crow's Nest Pass freight rate, doing whatever it did. And now it's gone. Now it's gone and everything has changed.

Singing the greys

Tuesday morning. It is grey. It is grey, grey, grey, grey, grey. It might as well be Tuesday evening. It has never been this grey this long. The sky is grey, the air is grey, the trees are grey, the ground is grey, the pavements are grey, the faces of people are grey, the lights left burning in the windows are grey. I am phoning in sick. I can't work today because I am grey. I will go to the doctor. He will give me something grey to take. He will tell me not to worry, things can't get any worse. But, he will say, things won't get any better.

When it is this grey, offices should shut down, stores should close, factories should pull the plugs on their assembly lines. Workers shouldn't be held responsible for shoddy workmanship when the weather is like this. Criminals shouldn't be held responsible for crimes. Parents who abandon their children should get letters from the government saying, "Congratulations, they had it coming." Churches should grant general absolution.

When it has been this grey for this long it is accepted by most knowledgeable authorities as a clear indication that the end is coming. It is a portent of doom.

Here are some others. (1) The temple will be torn down and there shall not be left one stone upon another that shall not be thrown down; (2) Nation shall rise against nation and kingdom against kingdom; (3) Great earthquakes shall be in diverse places, and famines and pestilences, and fearful sights and great signs shall there be from heaven; (4) Ye shall be betrayed both by parents, and brethren and kinfolks, and friends; (5) Ye shall see Jerusalem compassed with armies; and (6) There shall be signs in the sun, and in the moon, and in the stars; and upon the earth distress of nations with perplexity; the sea and waves roaring.

That's St. Luke quoting Jesus Christ. So take a look out the window.

Worse, take a look in yesterday's paper. There is a picture of Nancy Reagan planting a kiss on Santa at the White House. At the White House, Santa is played by that exemplar of good, clean violence, Mr. T. Nancy is planting a kiss on the shaved portion of Santa's Mohawk cut. Santa is wearing twenty-three pounds of gold and diamond jewelry. Nancy is sitting on his knee. She says her special holiday wish is that "everyone has peace."

Meanwhile, her hubby is turning plowshares back into swords. "With the best of intentions, we have tried turning our swords into plowshares, hoping others would follow. Well, our days of weakness are over."

Here endeth the days of weakness. "Military forces are back on their feet and standing tall." The Gospel according to John Wayne and Ronald Reagan.

What kind of peace does Nancy have in mind for us all to have some of? "Peace through strength," says Ronny. The world is so grey that outlines blur, everything shades together, foolishness and fools are no longer distinguishable against the background. When everything makes sense, nothing makes sense. There is nothing wrong with a policy of taking no prisoners, not when there won't be anybody left to do the taking. It's just common sense.

The other day I went up into the mountains of North York, followed the river valley that winds under Sheppard Avenue and around toward Bathurst Street. And I ascended a lofty ridge, taking as my route fluorescent-red-daubed surveyors' stakes that signal that soon these hills, too, will be brought low and turned into townhouses.

On top of the ridge, in a thick stand of trees, far from any dwelling and from any reason that a wayfarer could fathom, somebody had dug a great big hole, waist-deep and twice as long as a man and nearly as wide. The excavated dirt and rock was overgrown and the sides of the hole had long-since crumbled and fallen in.

Somebody had climbed into the woods and dug a great big hole.

He was probably seized with a raging flood of furious energy and had no idea on earth where to direct it, so he dug a hole and when he finished he slapped his hands together and said, "There, that's done." And he picked up his shovel and walked back down the hill.

I am calling in sick today, but I am not sick. It is a lie. I am out in the woods digging a great big hole. It is the only thing left to do.

6
Above the Crowd

Love that Larry

It was probably in the stars that I would finally fall in love. I just never considered the possibility it would be with a man, a thirty-three-year-old named Larry Walters who lives in San Pedro, California, and drives a truck for a living.

I began to fall for Larry when, in the grips of a lunacy so utter that he has never even attempted an explanation, he tied forty-five balloons filled with helium to the arms of a lawn chair, a plain, ordinary aluminum lawn chair, and rose 16,000 feet in the air. Sixteen thousand feet! That's 4,900 metres, 4.9 kilometres. That's more than three miles straight up! In a lawn chair!

But my feelings didn't turn to the purest love until he returned to earth and spoke the single greatest sentence in the history of adventure, of conquest, of man triumphant over his own frailty and the unspeakably indifferent forces of nature, until he, herald of anti-heroes, said: "I wouldn't do this again for anything."

Fired by ethereal inanity, the madman, Icarus-in-a-lawn-chair, slipped the silly bonds of earth and flew, not too near the sun but into the realms of satire and did not fall, but returned on wings of whimsy to take one banana step for mankind.

Because it is there? Mystical bombast. The Eagle has landed? Fatuous jingoism.

"I wouldn't do this again for anything."

Words to steal a heart. The salt of sanity to rub in the wounds of disdain we should inflict on all pompous adventurer-heroes who set themselves before us as godlike for their mastery over things that, when you get down to it, don't matter very much.

This has been on my mind because there is something about the Canadian Mount Everest expedition that rubs me a little wrong. In a blizzard of press-agentry these guys have set off as heroes-before-the-fact and their determination and courage is supposed to heat my chill, anaemic patriotism to a fervent, red-maple-leaf boil.

Come on. Climbing that mountain is old hat.

Women have climbed it. It has been climbed by busloads of Japanese tourists with Nikons around their necks. Now I'm instructed to feel some nationalistic, emotional involvement in an assault that sounds exactly like an assault, that sounds devoid of finesse or joy, that, if it succeeds, will succeed through sheer weight of numbers and material. It does not sound as if they intend to climb Mt. Everest so much as they intend to wear it down. It is about as exciting as watching a bulldozer doze.

We do have a craving for adventure. Over dinner I hear that a young doctor and his wife had the trip of a lifetime, ten days on the Colorado River, shooting the Grand Canyon aboard a rubber raft. And God knows some awesome adventures can befall individuals in circumstances that seem, at first, pretty banal. This spring a forty-three-year-old lawyer from Willowdale drowned while trying to canoe down the Don River. But hang gliders hang, windsurfers surf, the highways are jammed with bicycles and wheelchairs and runners going coast-to-coast, every one of them hell-bent to test his or her mettle.

In the Dirty Eighties, these are the equivalents of the six-day bike races and dance marathons of the Dirty Thirties. When everything else in the world is out of control, when it makes no sense at all and the air is filled with the sour-sweat smell of foreboding, these are the distractions people earnestly seek.

Or some do. It is curious that while hardly a day goes by without some pious adventurer testing his limits or risking his life, quite ordinary and reasonable folk get word that their limits are about to be tested, their lives risked, their hopes put in the fire as their jobs are lost, as plants and businesses close, as their savings evaporate and even macaroni becomes a luxury.

When living through the day is chancy, it is hard to dredge up wild admiration for those who take unnecessary chances, especially if they wrap their accomplishments in pride.

But it is possible to love a Larry Walters whose own stupefaction at what he had done was as great as anybody's. He attempted the ridiculous and achieved it.

Giving Daniel credit

The other day my friend Daniel Enright received an interesting letter from I.D. Sneddon, a group vice-president with Royal Trust.

"Dear Daniel Enright," the letter said. "We would like to extend a personal invitation to you to apply for the American Express Gold Card. The Gold Card provides you with an unparallelled array of personal services, designed to satisfy the lifestyle needs of successful people.

"For this reason, the Gold Card is unlike any other 'card.' It stands alone both in purpose and function. It is not only a flexible financial instrument, but it is also through its other unique benefits and privileges, a useful extension of one's normal access to service and value...."

Isn't that something? I.D. Sneddon, the group vice-president with Royal Trust, must have a pretty high opinion of my friend Daniel Enright to offer him an American Express Gold Card, which is to the ordinary American Express card as the sun is to a hockey puck.

I have a pretty high opinion of Daniel Enright myself. He is five years old and lives in a big old house in the west end with a mommy, a daddy, a dog named Daisy, a cat named Alexandre, and a brother named Anthony, who is one and a half and with whom Daniel shares a bunk bed. Daniel sleeps on the top bunk.

One of the best things about Daniel is he likes good jokes. Once he phoned me and said, "What goes ha-ha bump?"

I said, "I give up."

He said, "A man laughing his head off." Then we both laughed our heads off right there on the phone.

Now that he was being offered a flexible financial instrument by I.D. Sneddon, who is not just some nobody, but a group vice-president with Royal Trust, that would allow him free rein when it comes to satisfying his lifestyle needs, I thought it might be a good idea to drive out and interview him.

"Daniel," I said, "I would like to interview you."

"Oh, boy," he said.

"Why do you think Mr. Sneddon wants to give you an American Express Gold Card?" I asked.

Daniel looked perplexed. "Is this the interview?" he said.

"Yes," I said.

"Where's your microphone?" he said.

"I don't use a microphone. I listen to what you say and then I write it down in this notebook."

"Oh," said Daniel.

"Now, why do you think Mr. Sneddon wants to give you an American Express Gold Card?"

"It would be better with a microphone," said Daniel.

I moved on to the question of satisfying his lifestyle needs. It took a while to explain what a lifestyle was.

"Okay," he said, getting the drift, "I'd like to smoke cigarettes and drink beer and talk about girls."

"That's awful," I said. "Where'd you get ideas like that?"

"From you," he said.

But really it turns out that if Daniel had a lot of money he would buy bubble gum, a motorcycle for his dad, and a bicycle with training wheels.

"I'm old," he said. "I'm five. I can cross the road by myself and I can ride a bike."

Why did he think Mr. Sneddon wanted to give him all that credit – all that money? "Because if I had 1,600 moneys the banks would take it," he said. "The banks want to take all my money."

Daniel, I forgot to tell you, is in kindergarten. He calls it Grade Nothing. He was wearing a snappy pair of Snoopy pyjamas that were pin-striped like a Yankees' baseball uniform. He also had on a bright red Japanese kimono he calls his "happy coat."

"Listen, Daniel," I said, "this is all very well, but tell me, do you really know what an American Express Gold Card is?"

He nodded and looked wise. "What is it then?" I asked.

"You can't leave home without it," he said.

Terry passes

The pathetic fallacy was out of joint. The day of Terry Fox's death was not a cold, dark day, but sunny, breezy, and full of life.

The cottage yard was crowded with wildflowers – daisies that could be measured in bushels per acre, stands of bright, yellow hawkweed and deep orange devil's paintbrush; along the cedar-rail fence white choruses of wood anemone nodded vigorous agreement with the wind's slightest whim.

A chipmunk hardly big enough to fill a teacup explained that the front porch wasn't big enough for the both of us. A tribe of cedar waxwings, looking as fierce and sinister behind their black masks as a gang of Khyber bandits, plundered the bugs along the shore. Swallows by the dozens swooped and swerved, terns dove on minnows in the shallows, and a kingfisher, bristling with derring-do, fished with élan and éclat.

Things were jumping. And then arose a terrible, discordant racket. Four exuberant young men from up the road unveiled their proud new acquisition, an army surplus jeep that ground and snorted into view around the willows, rollicked over the gravel beach, and splashed into the bay to cheers and yahoos from its passengers.

The bay is not very deep and the jeep, reeking steam and exhaust, roared around and around in it, splashing and crashing, panicking the terns and giving flight to a graceful little green heron that had been searching curiously among the rocks on the point.

It drove me nuts. I immediately began compiling a list of grievances against youth: insensitive jerks, so self-centred they can't imagine that they have to share the planet with anyone else; lovers of noisy, stinking, graceless machines; defilers of the environment; no appreciation of what is appropriate, of what is in balance; compelled to leave their mark, however rough and scrawled, on anything they can find that is unmarked.

I got pretty harrumphy. But just when I was feeling most primly sensitive about my privacy, the radio brought news of Terry Fox's death, and I began to question my shrill, small perspective.

A few weeks ago my mother came to town, to Sunnybrook Hospital, to have a new hip installed. She had endured a winter of awful pain and was thoroughly frightened about the coming surgery. One night before the operation her apprehension threatened to boil over into panic and then, she said, "I thought about what I was going through and compared it to what Terry Fox was going through. I figured if he could handle it, I could handle it." She found that she couldn't be frightened any more.

Terry Fox made my mother brave.

I had found his accomplishments in his run and his perseverance so awesome that I couldn't relate to them in any real way. But this I could relate to. This I could see and touch and understand. This was a truly wonderful thing he did for me and mine.

By all accounts there was nothing specially remarkable about Terry Fox until fate marked him in such a ghastly way. By almost all accounts of heroism, heroes are remarkably ordinary until the chips go down and the hand is called.

That is maybe what moves us most about heroic deeds. They cause us to examine our own wells of ordinariness and leave us to wonder if, should the time ever come, there is anything within us that will rise to the challenge. Will we be able to meet the moment? And a lot of us doubt that we will be able to.

I looked out at the young men bashing and crashing about in the bay, so full of themselves and of life and of a sunny Sunday morning. They looked ordinary and yet who is to say that they might not some day be marked to dispense courage to the rest of us?

I no longer could complain about their momentary intrusion, or about any other gripes or grievances or burdens I am sometimes grimly aware I must bear. They all seemed petty.

Terry Fox has made it hard as hell to complain about anything.

I murmured the lines W.H. Auden wrote when William Butler Yeats died, and took a small liberty with them:

"Earth receive an honored guest,
Terry Fox is laid to rest."

There went Santa Claus

As policemen go, this one is perhaps more openly sentimental than most. For instance, he seemed genuinely sad that something as silly and carefree as the Santa Claus Parade should have caused him the worst moment in his career as a policeman.

He actually liked parade day, liked getting up and putting on his uniform in the dawn light and mustering downtown in what was often the first true cold of the year. He liked taking his place with the hundreds of other policemen assigned to stand at curbside to keep the crowd from doing whatever unimaginable things a crowd might do should it become overwhelmed by Santa's awesome progress.

He liked it because it wasn't often a policeman got to deal with so many people in such a simple good mood; not long before crowds usually called policemen pigs; a lot of times a policeman dealing with a crowd is dealing with drunkenness or anger or both.

Mostly he liked keeping an eye out for little kids who got stuck three, four, and five rows back and had their views blocked. That was pleasant work for a sentimental policeman, making sure little kids were allowed to slip around the adult legs to the front row so they could see Santa Claus go by.

It troubled him that the thing he looked forward to as much as anything each year was the thing that came as close as anything to causing him to resign. There was a profound irony in that; we had shared enough beers this aimless afternoon long after the fact to appreciate it. We urged him on with his story.

It was like this. He was standing there one Santa Claus Parade morning making sure little kids were allowed to slip around the adult legs to the front row when he spotted a tiny fellow, four or five years old, well back in the crowd. He edged people apart with his hands and gestured to the kid to come forward. The kid looked up at a man beside him, then back at the policeman, but continued to stand where he was. The policeman called to him. He said, "Hey, come on up here so you can see Santa Claus."

Again the kid looked at the man beside him. The man wore clothes that made the policeman think he was a latter-day hippie. He had a wide-brimmed leather hat on and wore his beard long. The man shook his head sharply at the little boy. The boy looked from him to the policeman and didn't move. The policeman was nonplussed.

The policeman turned back to the parade and the incident slipped from his mind. It slipped back first thing Monday morning when he was called into his unit commander's office and there, on chairs in front of the unit commander's desk, sat the bearded man and the little boy. The unit commander looked very cross. The policeman admitted to remembering the pair.

The unit commander asked the bearded man to repeat his complaint to the policeman. In a voice that made every word sound like a sneer, the man said he believed all capitalism was corrupt and wicked and he believed the biggest lie of capitalism was Santa Claus.

He had taught his son this and had taken him to the parade so the child could appreciate it for himself. This policeman had tried to undermine his teachings.

The policeman was amazed. He stammered, "I – I – I'm sorry you . . ."

The unit commander interrupted. He said the man didn't want an apology. "What does he want?" asked the policeman.

"He wants you to tell his son there is no Santa Claus," said the unit commander.

The policeman was horrified. For a minute he thought he was going to throw up. The commander repeated what he had said.

There was a heavy silence. The commander glared out the window. The policeman glared at his shoes. The father glared at the policeman. The little boy sat wide-eyed.

The policeman looked up at the boy. The policeman said, "There is no Santa Claus." The policeman turned and walked from the room. In the corridor he discovered he was crying.

Ah, Cisco!

To go back to the beginning, I was at a cocktail party when I met a man named Renaldo. "You're not by any chance related to the late Duncan Renaldo, are you?" I asked.

He said he was. He said he was Duncan Renaldo's nephew. "Ah, Cisco!" I shouted, and clapped him on the back with such bonhomie that he spewed a mouthful of gin and tonic over several beautiful people.

Imagine my excitement. *The Cisco Kid* was the very first television show I ever saw. Studies have proved that the first television show a child sees shapes his whole life, which explains why since the age of four I have spoken with a suave Spanish accent and my sombrero never gets knocked off in a fistfight.

Now here was a blood link to the actor who played my idol. I hung on Renaldo's arm and trumpeted his glory.

Renaldo, a modest man and not accustomed to such celebrity, kept trying to duck out of the room, but I was determined that he receive his due. "Stop hanging on my arm," he hissed.

"Stop hanging on his arm," his wife hissed the next morning at breakfast. "We can't afford another mouth to feed and, besides, you hog all the covers."

At a party a few nights later I met a man in the radio game. While I hate name-droppers, I couldn't resist mentioning that I knew Duncan Renaldo's nephew. "He's my very best friend," I said.

The man in the radio game was transfixed. "Ah, Cisco!" he shouted, and clapped me on the back with such bonhomie that I spewed a mouthful of guacamole over several beautiful people. All that night he dragged me from group to group, trumpeting my fortune in having, as a best friend, Duncan Renaldo's nephew.

He insisted that I appear on his phone-in radio show. At first I was reluctant, but after a brief financial discussion, I was persuaded that it was something I ought to share with the world.

He introduced me to the listeners as "my best friend in the whole world, a really sweet guy whose best friend is Duncan Renaldo's nephew." The response was tremendous. Phone circuits were blown out all the way to the Arctic Circle.

You know how you hear about someone who is rich and famous, pursued by women as tempting as blueberry muffins, a power in the world of show business, and you wonder how it all began? In my case it was one of those lucky breaks.

Johnny Carson – would you believe it! – was driving through town that night on his way to emcee a stag and just happened to have his radio on. He stopped at a phone booth and called the station. Johnny said I absolutely had to fly to Los Angeles (he said L.A.) the next night and be his lead-off guest.

I didn't want to leave Canada, but it's the old story: there's only so far you can go this side of the border. Ask Lorne Greene. He said as much when he stopped by the house for dinner last night.

The show drew the highest ratings of Johnny's career.

I related anecdote after anecdote about Duncan Renaldo and his nephew and our lives together. The rapport was so warm that Johnny told Charo and Steve Martin and Dr. Joyce Brothers to stay backstage in the green room because it would be a waste having other guests on that night.

Not long after I was asked back to be the guest host while Johnny was off doing a bar mitzvah in Duluth and – this has all been documented in *People* magazine – one thing just sort of led to another. Marie wanted me to replace Donny. Cher wanted me to replace everybody. And there was the feud with Barbra after we did the album together and – listen, I was really embarrassed about it – I got the Grammy and she didn't.

Right now we're negotiating with Francis Ford Coppola for a movie based on my autobiography, *The Legend and The Legend*. I see De Niro as me; Redford is too Waspish to handle the Spanish accent.

And the other night you probably saw the *Battle of the Superstars* where I easily beat the guy whose brother-in-law was Guy Madison's (Wild Bill Hickock, remember?) barber in watermelon seed spitting, mud wrestling, and chugalugging beer. My own series starts taping in the spring.

You probably wonder – everybody does – do you forget your old friends when you climb to the top? Not me. If I ever get back to Toronto I plan to look up Renaldo, my oldest and dearest friend.

The coal mine's ghosts

The story has it that mother's grandfather was a shift foreman of great heart in the collieries of Sydney Mines on Cape Breton. The men who worked for him, as did most of the miners there around the turn of the century, laboured in an economy that is no stranger to that part of the country. They worked – if they could get work – numbingly long hours in wretched circumstances and made enough money to live in poverty.

As foreman, mother's grandfather made a bit more money than his men and he would stop with them for a glass of whisky on paynight. His men would have seen their pay already gone to pay bills for groceries already eaten and so great was his heart and the charity of the whisky that he would take whatever money he had and divide it up among them. When he got home he would have none left for his own family.

To overcome this fiscal obstacle, the family sought a supplementary source of income and began to breed and raise pit canaries. Pit canaries were ordinary canaries that were taken down in the mine to sing their hearts out. When the canary's song stopped and the poor creature fell dead from its perch, the miners knew that the gas – the damp, they called it – was rising and they had to run or die themselves.

The family, not least of them mother's grandfather, industriously raised a wonderful flock of canaries, which were kept in an aviary behind the house. The story has it that one paynight mother's grandfather came home and peered for the longest time through the wire at the trilling, flitting birds. So great was his heart and the charity of the whisky that finally he said, "Och, ye poor wee things," and opened the cage door and let them all go.

Mother's father was a tiny man, a splendid soccer player who had a hundred girlfriends, one of whom he married and she was the

117

daughter of the shift foreman of such great heart.

Grandpa also worked in the coal mines at Sydney Mines and as hateful as the work was, there was one thing he hated above all else and that was the darkness. All week long the men would descend into the pit before the sun rose in the morning and they would make their way to the coal face miles out under the Atlantic. When their shift ended and the hoist returned them to the surface, the sun would have set. The light would be gone. The night of his life seemed interminable.

He had one wish: to find a way to take his family somewhere the sun shone.

The only time Grandpa's night was broken was Sunday. One Sunday he and his wife heard a truly amazing man speak, the Reverend Billy Sunday, a man who had been a baseball star and who would slide across the stage on his stomach to show how you got to the home plate of Heaven, a man who could rage against booze at 300 words a minute, a legendary evangelist who brought more than a million souls down the sawdust trail to Christ.

He brought at least two of them that day in Cape Breton. It must have been the most exciting thing they had ever heard or seen. Billy Sunday and his simple – perhaps too simple – Gospel brought hope for life everlasting to people whose lives seemed exceedingly finite. It was something to cling to, something more than nothing. Grandpa didn't miss the words of the hymn that promised a morning that breaks eternal, bright and clear.

Well, time passed and the damp got into his lungs and he was sent to a tuberculosis sanitorium in Ontario and, finally, he and his brood settled in Guelph. He is long dead now, but for years I heard stories of the collieries of Sydney Mines where he laboured in the unrelenting dark and made his simple wish. No matter how much I heard, I couldn't imagine what it was like.

A week ago I learned a little bit. I was given a helmet and a lamp and a cape to cover my shoulders and was lowered in the hoist of the Princess Colliery at Sydney Mines, 620 feet down the shaft that Grandpa descended every day some seventy years ago.

We were led on a tour by a wry old miner who spent thirty-one years underground in the Princess Colliery until 1976 when the last rake of cars brought the last ton of coal from the face six miles out under the ocean and the mine closed. "Work as if your life depends on it," said a sign we passed, "because your life depends on it."

But I missed a lot of what our guide said because I was listening to other things, to silent things whirring beyond the gleams of our little lamps, to ghosts and the comradely murmurings of men of great heart who knew brutal work but who struggled and went on to the timeless daylight of their home beyond the shore.

Standing in the darkness, I wasn't at all afraid.

Longevity is reward of dissolute

Theory No. 1. The James F. Fixx Theory. Jim Fixx was the celebrated jogger who wrote *The Complete Book of Running* in which he advanced the claim that a person who jogged would live longer. Fixx died recently while jogging. He was only fifty-two.

Many people concluded from Fixx's demise that running was bad for you, something they had suspected all along. My theory is that running is bad for you, not because it is bad for you as its critics insist, but because it is good for you, as Fixx's death proves.

An autopsy revealed that Fixx died of congestive heart failure and that his death might have been forestalled had he undergone a by-pass operation, something that is fairly straightforward nowadays.

Had Fixx not been out running and keeping fit he would have sat in front of his television set and smoked and got fat. He would have felt awful and gone to his doctor, who would have diagnosed his heart disease and repaired it. Instead, Fixx was in such good shape it never occurred to anyone that his heart was on the verge of going blooey until it did.

If you want to live a long time, live a life of dissolution, one that is sedentary, high on calories, rolling in cholestrol. Then you will be at your physician's all the time and will get advance warning of the crippling things about to befall you, and you will thus benefit from the amazing, life-prolonging advances in medical science.

Theory No. 2. The Fifty-Cents-A-Litre-For-Gasoline Theory. The other day I paid 49.7 cents a litre for regular gasoline. Unleaded and super grades have already broken the fifty-cent barrier and one of these days regular gas will, too. The petroleum companies worry that the fifty-cent price might have a negative return in terms of consumption, that psychologically we might rebel and cut down on our driving.

In the early 1970s the Ontario government kept bumping up taxes on cigarettes until the price for a pack of twenty was nudging $1. The Treasury worried that when the price hit $1 so many people would refuse to pay it and quit smoking that there would be a net tax loss to the province. They even kept the price down for a time to avoid such a negative return. But finally they closed their eyes and pulled the trigger and shot the taxes up. So far as can be determined, the increase didn't affect a single smoker's level of consumption. This morning a pack of twenty is selling for $2.45 at my local variety store and $2.50 is in sight.

Government feels obliged to take moral positions, to get onside with the angels. It should be seen to encourage people to stop smoking, to drink in moderation, and should condemn the evils of tobacco and booze to body and soul. It should encourage conservation and sensible energy use, both to keep our fuel supplies from petering out and to keep the air we breathe from turning to fudge.

But it could never afford to advocate these high-toned moral things without the revenue from tobacco and liquor and gasoline taxes. Were it not for the wages of vice, the government could never espouse virtue. If we start to balk at fifty-cent gas or $2.50 packages of cigarettes or $20 cases of beer, then the government won't have the wherewithal to tell us these things are bad for us.

Beside such fiscal considerations, politics has a few well-chosen words to say. The flue-cured tobacco growers are blue because so many people are quitting smoking and getting healthy that the farmers can't sell their crop. The Niagara grape farmers are causing a ruckus because 30,000 tonnes of grapes are going begging because of want of demand for wine. And when have the petroleum companies and service station operators not been moaning about something or other? Substantial constituencies, these.

If you add to them all their allied industries, you will see that there is hardly a segment of the country that wouldn't be severely damaged if we started to do what was good for us and lived healthy, moderate, responsible lives.

My theory is that if we want to keep the country strong, vibrant, and full of high purpose, the only way to do it is by living lives of dissolution and waste, lives that are irresponsible and extravagant. This theory, on a macro-scale, is remarkably close to Theory No. 1 as it relates to an individual's well-being. I think I might be on to something.

Amicus

The cat was having a nervous breakdown. Every time I stood up or picked something up or made a sudden move it scrunched down on its belly and slithered frantically into hiding. It was as if after a long association in which it took me for granted I had become a monster, a fiend, the Cat Destroyer.

It was spooked and it had me spooked, because I was in fact a fiend. I was going to get rid of the cat. I believe cats have particularly sensitive antennae when it comes to picking up human feelings. The cat had my number.

The cat's name was Amicus, Latin for "friend." It got the name because it was friendly, almost intolerably so. It was not a peaceful, dozing lap cat. It was a nuzzling, kneading, rubbing, never-still creature that drooled all over you like a purring faucet.

Now it cowered and fled the way animals do that have been beaten, kicked, regularly ill-used. It was doing this so I would think twice about getting rid of it. Anybody who got this cat and saw it behave like that would assume its previous human had subjected it to cruel abuse. Maybe used it for medical experiments. Did I want to be seen as that kind of human? I was being subjected to cat blackmail, to black catmail.

It had to go. Someone had been allergic to it for a long time. We can live with some allergies. A little flak, a little static, a few gristly bits are part of life. Sometimes we're bothered by things we care for and we live with them because we care for them. Except that over the years these allergies grew worse, became full-blown asthma, contributed to an apparently chronic bronchitis.

We kept putting it off. Maybe one of these days the allergy would disappear. Maybe we would find somebody who would take the cat and love him for what he was. We kept asking. There were no takers.

It is not easy to find somebody who wants a ten-year-old cat. The trouble with a ten-year-old cat is it is not a kitten. It is not cute and playful and careless of the morrow. It has views; it is set in its ways. Besides, this cat was dumb. For example, it never figured out the out-of-doors. The odd time it could be persuaded to go outside it would languish by the door in agony until you let it back inside to use the litter box. Do you think anybody could explain just how ridiculous that was? Do you think it would listen?

121

And it had a personality disorder stemming from never coming completely to grips with its sex-change operation. That is doubtless a hard thing to come to grips with, and there are no cat counsellors listed in the Yellow Pages. It started off as a boy but, because of certain problems with its urinary tract that I don't like to think about for various personal reasons, it was replumbed and became a girl. At least in theory.

In practice it was left with a psychological short-circuit. Often at night I was startled awake as it made noisy and energetic (and drooling) love to my foot. When you emerge from nightmare that way you think neither too clearly nor too sympathetically of a sorely troubled cat. All you have is the terrifying realization that Something Awful is happening to your foot and you Flinch! mightily and a Thing goes hissing and squalling through the air and there is yelling and thrashing and recriminations.

And it was fat. The great wrinkly folds of its tomcat haunches were unfillable. When food was on its mind – and it wasn't in one of the neurotic bursts of the psy-war that had commenced between us – it was loving and drooling and wouldn't let you alone. Utter dependence was seldom so cloyingly displayed.

A ten-year-old cat, plain striped alley variety, requiring daily medication to keep its plumbing open, dumb as could be, and a weirdo, wasn't easy to get rid of. Even the Humane Society wouldn't put him up for adoption. He was simply too old, the man at the counter said. And the alternative was sad as sad could be.

I think that for a long time Amicus had sensed what an unfair fate held in store for him. He was uncharacteristically still as I held him, as we signed a form, as we paid the $9 fee, as an attendant came from the back and took him away.

And us? We went out and stood in the alley beside the animal shelter and in the noonday sun we wept.

Moral: none.

A grump afoot

A ragged, blustery morning. Octoberish. Sunlight glances sporadically through rips in the clouds. I waken thinking any day now the fish will be jumping and the cotton will be high, but the weatherman on the radio tells me there was frost in the outlying regions. It is enough to frost anybody's outlying regions, I tell the weatherman, and get up anyway.

North I head, and west. Up in the northwest corner of the metropolis Finch Avenue ends with a bang at Islington and the Humber streams beneath their intersection. I slink upstream along the river bank with a querulous eye peeled for summery thoughts.

It used to be said of joggers – and maybe it still is; people are prepared to say just about anything of joggers, and I'm prepared to believe it – that they were running away from things, from aging, from death, from plodding reality. So far as a jogger's fight-or-flight instinct was concerned, flight held the reins. (Coming up to the office on the elevator a little while ago a man told me he didn't jog because jogging jiggled the brain loose. I believed that, too.)

When I slink off to follow a river on a workaday morning I sometimes wonder if I'm not making a similar flight. Perhaps my journey is not one of discovery, as I like to think, but of avoidance. Then I saw in the paper that the world will spend $1 trillion on arms next year and I concluded that if avoidance had ever been my objective it was no longer. With that much new bang-bang added to what the world already has strapped on its hip there's nowhere you can go to avoid anything. There is no place left to hide. (And what, for God's sake, is a trillion?)

One thing we might do, I suppose, is curl up in quivering balls of paranoia. But another has to do with something a friend of mine says he is discovering about the tyranny of choice. The world is so much with my friend I wonder that he doesn't crumple under the strain, but he doesn't because, he says, he can't.

He can't because he has obligations that leave him no choice but to soldier on. His discovery that he had no choice was, he says, liberating. The pressures eased. A lot of static was tuned out of his mind. When there is no hiding place there is no need to worry about hiding. So why not stop worrying about it and just go for a walk? If the world wants to shoot me, it knows where to find me.

The marsh marigold is in bloom, blasts of yellow creating their own light in the wet shadows. Above the river, hordes of rough-winged swallows sweep, vacuuming up the insects that insist on hatching despite the chill. When nature says "marsh marigold" or "rough-winged swallow" it says exactly what it means. Nature is always open and aboveboard. None of this "peaceful" that means "warlike" or "life" that means "death."

Grump, grump, grump. The river meanders here through hairpin curves. This is called Rowntree Mills Park and patches of it have been left overgrown and wild. Pheasants are croaking lustily. In the low branches of the overhanging willows a pair of red-wing blackbirds make love in the old fashioned way, oblivious of a wandering voyeur.

Above all throbs a mechanical racket. I follow it and see, across the river, a yellow bulldozer scraping earth. It looks like the birth labours of a subdivision on what had been a perfectly good river bank. It fills me with gloom. It could well be that a track left by a bulldozer is every bit as representative of God's footprints as a violet's bloom, but sometimes God's feet are big and muddy and leave an awful mess.

I cross the river on a footbridge (the swallows are daredevils, they do barrel rolls under it) and encounter a man piloting a Metro Parks golf cart along a track toward the bulldozer. I flag him down and ask what's going on. Is it a subdivision?

"No," he says, "this is flood-control land. It's part of the park. Nobody can build here. They can't build everywhere, thank Christ. The bulldozer is doing some grading and drainage work. We're making this part of the park more accessible."

Imagine that. A bulldozer doing good works. In my notebook I write, "Expanding park. Faith restored. Permanently? Too soon to tell."

7
T.O.

Positively Orwellian

A lot of fuss is being made over George Orwell, the dead writer, the one who wrote *Nineteen Eighty-Four*, but next to no attention is being paid to the other George Orwells, the living ones, who, just because they didn't necessarily write *Nineteen Eighty-Four*, don't deserve to be overlooked in this, the big Orwell year.

There are fourteen George Orwells listed in the Metro telephone directory, fifteen if you count the George Orwell Association of Toronto, sixteen if you count George Orwell Dry Cleaners.

"It sure is something," said George Orwell, a retired stationary engineer who lives on Sherbourne Street. "Especially with all this publicity. I must get asked to speak two, three times a month. Just last night I was at the Lions Club. I told their activities chairman I wasn't George Orwell, the dead writer. He said it didn't matter, all they wanted was a body to get up and say a few words after dinner. So I gave them twenty minutes on hanging around with Ernest Hemingway."

"Ernest Hemingway?"

"Yup. Me and Ernie worked twenty-nine years for the school board. Together we switched them boilers from coal-fired to oil-fired. Then we'd go down to the Legion and play darts. After about three beers, Ernie'd forget to let go of the dart. He'd shoot, but it'd stay clenched in his fingers and whang around and stick in his thigh on the follow-through. He was quite a guy, Ernie.

"Anyway, I gave the Lions twenty minutes of this and then asked if there was any questions, and there wasn't. So they gave me this bottle of rye and said I was welcome back any time."

The next George Orwell I met was a high school chemistry teacher in Etobicoke. He said he was sure he'd read something by George Orwell at some time or other, maybe in college, but he couldn't exactly remember. I asked if any curious or humorous things happened to him because their names were the same.

"Whose?" he asked.

"Yours and George Orwell's," I said.

"Say," he said, "you're right. I never thought about it before. I can't wait to get home and tell the wife. She'll get a big kick out of it. On second thought, maybe I won't tell her. She already gets quite a few phone calls asking her to send somebody around to pick up their dirty clothes. She says its a plain nuisance having the same name as George Orwell Dry Cleaners. If she finds out we also have the same name as George Orwell, the dead writer, she would get pestered half crazy with phone calls for him."

I went to a meeting of the George Orwell Association of Toronto, an organization devoted to helping people whose names are George Orwell keep themselves straight from one another and from George Orwell, the dead writer. The president of the George Orwell Association is (are?) George and George Orwell, identical twins who are also (is also?) owner of George Orwell Dry Cleaners.

While the George Orwell who was wearing a brown suit and a blue necktie presided over a meeting of seven or eight George Orwells dressed in brown suits and blue neckties, his identical twin brother, George, dressed in a brown suit and a blue necktie, told me their parents had been unable to tell them apart and so had called them both George. They were named after a dear cousin of their mother's who had gone to school at Eton and then joined the police force in India or Burma or someplace. "Mom lost touch with her cousin after that."

The brothers had gone into the dry-cleaning business because, as they were so used to having their clothes mixed up, they thought it was an experience they might profitably offer to other people named George Orwell. "It's a specialized sort of service, you might say," he said. "But lately business has been falling off. We think a competing George Orwell is intercepting our phone calls.

I asked if the association ever discussed the works of George Orwell, and co-president George Orwell said, "Regularly. In fact, tonight George Orwell, the house painter, is delivering a paper on the Hemingway-Orwell letters, something he knows all about since Ernest Hemingway, the stationary engineer, sends him all his letters

126

to George Orwell, the stationary engineer, by mistake. Stick around. It should be good."

Fixing the old place up

Toronto is too flat. I have recently been travelling in mountains and can vouch for the wonderful character mountains give the face of the land. If you look across Toronto, past the buildings – which are all we have by way of real heights – you can see clear to the other side. You can see to the end right from the beginning. There's not much drama in that.

A mountain or two, a snow-capped peak raking the sky at Yonge and Adelaide or at Kennedy and Sheppard, would add some variety. But if snow-capped peaks are a bit too major an undertaking, I would settle for some honest-to-goodness hills.

Some say the city already has hills. There's a hill on Avenue Road and there's the Pottery Road hill, but these and the others like them are just the edges of old watercourses and prehistoric lakes. They're not hills you can climb and, when you reach the top, look all around and feel you are the monarch of all that you survey.

There's even a part of town that calls itself, very grandly, Silver Hills. It's up there south of Highway 401 and west of Bayview. There's a bus that wends there with a destination sign on it that reads, without a trace of a blush, "Silver Hills."

I rode it once because I wanted to get a look at these alleged hills – I suspected they were oversold – and was no more disappointed than any rube who pays his ninety-five cents to get into the sideshow tent to see "The Seven Wonders of the World" and ends up watching Alvin Wonder play the ukulele while his wife sings and their five children form a human pyramid.

I've played pool on tables that had more rolls than Silver Hills.

Don't fool yourself into thinking Toronto's terrain offers any more than a few folds and crinkles to a man who's seen real hills. What we want is a dark and brooding hill, one whose wooded flanks loom against the horizon, or even better, a range of hills like that.

Come to think of it, Toronto's rivers run too straight. For the most part they make a bee-line down to the lake as if they can hardly wait to get through town. For all their inclination toward lingering for a chat, you'd think they didn't want to be seen in our company.

What we need are some rivers with big, sweeping bends that swirl through the city, that meander and wind. When you curl up on a riverbank to examine life's possibilities through a hazy afternoon, you don't want to curl up beside a river that appears to be on an errand. It sets your mind to thinking that maybe there's someplace important you're supposed to be, too.

I wouldn't mind a broader river, either. One about a quarter-mile across that started somewhere up in the northwest and hit town about York University, then sashayed down, back and forth across Yonge Street a couple of times, and emptied into the lake out near Greenwood Racetrack would be ideal. You'd need some real bridges, substantial ones, suspension bridges, across a river like that. And there'd be a fair amount of river traffic, tugs towing barges, and likely a shipyard.

That would be a mighty river. A river like that would give Toronto character to spare. I don't know a good reason why we shouldn't get one.

While these hills and rivers are being installed, it would be a good time to do something about the shoreline. Toronto's shoreline is too cut and dried. It's as if God ran out of creativity the day he was designing it and just drew it in with a ruler.

There's not a bay on it worth the name. To give it even a touch of distinction, we've been building long, skinny spits out from it. What we need is a good, big bay. One the size of Fundy might be more than we can handle, but I'm sure there are economy-size models that would suit our needs.

And some fjords would be appreciated. Rocky, rugged fjords swept by the tides. They could become Toronto's hallmark. Of course, then we'll need some tides. This could be handled nicely if we got rid of Lake Ontario and replaced it with an ocean. There's a lot of character to be gained from an ocean.

I can see it all now. Toronto's purple hills, her bustling rivers, her wave-swept ocean shore.

When we finally get the geography fixed up, we can start to work on the weather.

The Rosedale bus

When you arrive at the Rosedale station you know right away you are about to ride a first-class bus. You enter the station through ornate bronze doors cast in Florence during the Renaissance and depicting the history of public transit all the way back to Charon and his Stygian boat.

The ticket-taker is the scion of one of the city's leading families. After taking your fare he directs you through the exquisite Louis XIV turnstiles where you are met by a glamorous hostess who takes you to the Rosedale bus lounge and offers you champagne and canapés and fluffy slippers to wear while you wait.

The bus pulls in and is surrounded by a squad of men who scrub its tires and wipe its windows and polish its already-brilliant chromework with the finest flannel, imported from Europe.

The driver steps down. The eyes of children light up at the sight of his heroic figure. The driver of the Rosedale bus wears riding boots that gleam like black suns and jodhpurs and carries a riding crop which he flicks against his calf. Around his neck hang golden chains. A coiffeur fusses over his hair so it will be perfect when he departs.

The ladies who board the Rosedale bus wear furs of animals so rare they can only be trapped by magicians deep in the mountains on the other side of the world. The men who make their way to the contoured seats read nothing but the financial sections of the newspaper and can buy and sell the likes of you and me.

Even the rougher sorts among the passengers would not be found on buses anywhere else but in Rosedale. They wear silk shirts unbuttoned to the navel and their tattoos are not serpents and daggers but signed originals by Chagall and Warhol and Bosch.

When the bus slips out of the station a loud cheer goes up from the crowd of well-wishers gathered on the platform to wish it bon voyage. The air is filled with coloured streamers and confetti and the lieutenant-governor is on hand to wave good-bye.

The bus swings east, its fabled journey begun at last. It is preceded on foot by scores of maidens from private schools who strew its path with rose petals. Its fuel has been laced with perfume by Arpeges so the exhaust will not give offence to the tasteful souls who inhabit the fine mansions it must pass.

The air becomes so sweet with the scent of crushed rose petals and the seductive perfume that birds flying behind the bus grow drunk on the fragrance and fly straight up, beyond the stratosphere, to expire in the breathless eternity among the distant stars.

The bus turns north, makes its majestic way across a bridge, under the over-arching maples that bathe its course in the velvet half-light of Bay Street boardrooms, past the fine mansions, not one of which has fewer than forty rooms. The mansions are staffed with efficient domestics each of whom apprenticed under a crowned head after taking a master's degree in business administration. When the bus comes to a mansion that has fewer than forty rooms or a staff hired from the classified sections of the newspaper, the driver will turn around and go some other way. In an age of nouveau suburbia, the Rosedale bus maintains its standards.

It is much the same when the Rosedale bus approaches a bus stop where people are waiting who are obviously without pedigrees. "Drive on! Drive on!" the passengers shout. As the bus rumbles past the stop they cast a cultured eye upon the parvenus and joke to one another, "Let them take taxis."

With the silver-bell laughter that marks the residents of Rosedale, they make their way along the Persian carpets in the aisle toward the dance floor in the back and there, under a shimmering chandelier of Waterford crystal, they foxtrot to the mellow strains of the twenty-five-piece orchestra provided for their entertainment, or perhaps they take a sauna or swim in the Olympic-sized pool.

The bus loops and swirls through the intricate maze of plush streets and never once leaves Rosedale. It is not just a first-class bus, it goes first-class all the way.

Wild bicycles

A lot of bicycles have been sighted in the last couple of days. They have been sighted in High Park, on Spadina Avenue, on Merton Street, on (bravely!) Yonge Street, and tethered to lamp posts in Kensington Market and to a tree that grows through a hole in the concrete in front of our office.

The number of reported sightings would be negligible if it were August. More bicycles run down strollers on the boardwalk in the Beaches in a half hour on Thanksgiving weekend than have been sighted in the whole of the city in February. But, for February, we certainly have a lot of bicycles and bicycle-watchers are just about beside themselves.

Bicycles usually hibernate in winter. They burrow into a dark corner of the basement, slip out of gear, and dream month-long dreams of long downhills and travelling with a wind that is always at their backs.

When they are suddenly hauled out at this time of year they have a startled, dazed look and can turn surprisingly skittish at the sight of a patch of snow, or ice on the bricks between the streetcar tracks. They look a little put-upon, what with the unaccustomed weight of heavy coat, mitts, and scarf pulled up over the rider's nose and hat pulled down over the rider's ears.

There is no little concern that this freakish, mild weather is not terribly good for bicycles. If they are forced to bloom now, tricked out of their restorative winter rest by a false spring, will they shrivel and blacken when the real cold finally does hit? Will they suffer a premature autumn and be strewn around, so many rotting rusted hulks, when the real summer comes?

I wonder whether man, as he continues to bend nature to his own selfish ends, will cause the bicycle to finally become extinct, just as he finally destroyed the wringer washer and the yardstick.

I think that when man began to domesticate the bicycle, he sealed the bicycle's doom.

My grandfather has told me stories of coming to this country to escape the oppressions of Europe and to carve a new life out of the untrammelled wilderness. They settled in what we now call Rosedale and he felled trees and squared the timbers and, with the help of his sons, painstakingly constructed a rough, twenty-three room mansion. They scraped a meagre existence out of the unforgiving Toronto Stock Exchange; slowly they tamed the savage bond market and ventured warily into speculation on railroad rights-of-way.

He said, and I have no reason to doubt him, that in those days vast herds of wild bicycles roamed freely across the open hillsides and swarmed through the ravines. They were a sight to see, the sunlight glinting off their spokes, their crossbars strong, their pedals spinning in a mighty blur.

The horizon was black with them, he said. In the fall, when they migrated toward the basements where they hibernated, it sometimes took a week for a single herd to pass a given spot. Whole towns would turn out to witness the incredible processions and the towns-folk would stand mute with awe at their grandeur. Wheel on wheel they would come, endlessly rolling.

It was too grand to last, of course. Soon professional hunters,

131

armed with combination padlocks and case-hardened steel chains, would lie along the bicycle trails and pick off stragglers. It became a mark of distinction to have your own bicycle. The King of Denmark wanted a new one every year. Teddy Roosevelt was photographed riding one.

Eventually the demand was too great. The herds were decimated, finally gone completely; nothing was left but dim grandfatherly memories, faded images in the Stereopticon. The hissing sound that wakes us in the night is merely the wind, not the whisper of millions of tires rolling in majesty across the plain.

And look at the poor bicycle today. Not even left in peace through the winter but dragged, docile and forlorn, out to service our whim and the freakishness of the weather.

I went down to the bicycle room in the basement of my building and edged along the ranks of dozing machines until I found mine, propped at an angle and perfectly still under a layer of dust. The tires were soft and the brake cables had lost their tension.

For a crazy moment I considered waking it and taking it out to some open, wild space – the parking lot at Yorkdale, for instance – and saying, "Go, my beauty. Take your freedom and race across the world. I am returning you to your beginnings."

But I didn't. It couldn't live without me. Sleep gently.

A walk on the mild side

The walking tours of Toronto, which begin in May and run into October, promise to be fair hikes, full to the brim with scenic wonders, pertinent facts, and historic significance – heavy going if you're not in shape. To tune up I took a shorter, less presumptuous walk: from the side entrance of my apartment building to our local milk store, the Daily Food Mart, some fifty steps across the way.

The walk bisects Pailton Crescent midway on its S-shaped course between Merton Street and Balliol Street, which are named after Oxford colleges and lend an intellectual tone to a neighbourhood already slumped under the weight of brains listening to the morning news and weather in the high-rise apartments that provide most of the scenery.

Balliol is properly pronounced BALE-yul, but if you say BALE-yul you'll never get a pizza delivered or find a taxi driver who knows what on earth you're talking about. If you want to sound like a native, say Buh-LOIL. Merton is pronounced Merton.

One night I saw the owner of the milk store on television. He was being interviewed in connection with the Korean airliner that was shot down. His role was that of spokesman for the Korean community. It pulls you up a bit short to discover that the man who owns your local milk store has a second, celebrity life as a spokesman. It makes you realize you're much better connected to world events than you thought.

Beside the store are tennis courts and beside them, on the corner, a silvery metallic structure that most people in the neighbourhood think is a hydro installation or something to do with public works, a pumping station perhaps. It is shaped like a couple of horizontal packing crates.

Imagine my surprise when I learned (by reading a plaque) that it is art, a sculpture in stainless steel by someone named Kosso Eloul. If Kosso Eloul ever decides to give up starving in a garret, he could make a tidy income designing hydro installations and pumping stations. He has the touch.

Nearby is a tangled pile of tree limbs that brought down some power lines in the big wind this week. While the storm was at its most rambunctious, Hydro crewmen used chainsaws to clear things away. It shows that the awesome power of nature reaches even into this part of town. As if more proof were needed, once, right where the pile is now, I saw an albino squirrel.

I followed it south (if you want a break from routine, there's nothing like following an albino squirrel) until it disappeared into the brush and trash that clog what was once the Belt-line Railway right-of-way, bordering Mount Pleasant Cemetery. You can just glimpse it through the trees, beyond the lot where those old clunkers of cars are rusting away.

Three of those cars – one a convertible, in fact – are Corvairs. What a car the Corvair was, rear-engined, sporty. It was the car that started Ralph Nader raiding; he wrote *Unsafe At Any Speed* about it. You might say the Corvair ignited the whole modern consumer movement. Before it came along we drove any old thing, ate any old thing, drank any old thing, breathed any old thing, and died like flies.

Just beyond the store a modern office building is being completed. Before it went up a long, low rock 'n' roll bistro called the Clubhouse occupied the site. In its latter months, the Clubhouse specialized in

Wet T-Shirt Nites, but it went under anyway. Any business that can't be rescued by Wet T-Shirt Nites simply can't be rescued.

Around the corner on Merton are the nine magnificent concrete silos of the Dominion Coal and Wood Co., building suppliers whose name conjures up a time when every boy knew the difference between bituminous and anthracite. During winter breaks the Dominion yardmen cluster around a fire of lumber scraps that whips and roars in a corroded oil drum.

Sometimes, when I'm not in a rush, I'll toddle along from the store a few yards to the smallest park in town. It is two granite boulders, six tatty pines, and a bench. Hardly room enough to unwrap a sandwich. I'll sit and watch pigeons make frantic circles in the sky, sniff the exhaust fumes, drift a bit, dream. Unless the bench is already occupied, in which case I get on with my business.

Nothing finer than Spadina

The brunch crowd is gathering on the shaded portico of the Scott Mission. A man with a patriarchal white beard and wearing a beret and a blue denim apron sweeps the sidewalk in front of the Canadian Imperial Bank of Commerce at Spadina and College with a kitchen broom. The bank is not yet open.

When he finishes he props the broom on his shoulder and crosses College to inspect the front-end loader and the back-hoe idling in front of the Crest Grill. The machines had been digging up the storm sewer, but their operators are on their break. The bearded man circles each machine slowly, as if they are models in a showroom and he, a customer, is imagining the wonders he might perform if he could exchange his broom for one of them.

The Crest has a new front. For years it looked as if someone started to tear it down and then wandered off and forgot. But the sign overhanging the street is the old one. Looking closely you can see that the name was once Crescent – the t in Crest is painted over the old, second c and the rest of the word painted out. Now, as it fades, Crescent begins to reappear. This effect is called "pentimento."

Lillian Hellman wrote an autobiography called *Pentimento*. In May of 1952 she wrote a letter to the U.S. House Committee on Unamerican Activities saying, "I cannot and will not cut my conscience to fit this year's fashions." In May of 1973 I fell in love. We walked all night and at dawn had breakfast of fried salami and scrambled eggs in the Crest Grill. In May of 1984 I ease down a broad city street, a searcher after rhythms and patterns, trying to discern shapes in a terrain where none might exist except in the imagination.

A waitress in a red corduroy apron comes out of the Coffee Stop to stand in the sun while she eats orange sections. She has red fingernails. A fat man in a red shirt comes out of ABC Cash & Carry carrying a black dog with hair that hangs over its eyes in ringlets.

Men unload yellow cages scrunched full of white chickens from a truck backed into a bay at the Toronto Packing Co. In the next bay men load a truck with cases of eggs. Walking south on Spadina this humid morning, the chickens come first, and then the eggs.

The chicken smell is cloying as smoke. I close my eyes and see the chickens behind my grandparents' long-ago house, hens scratching beyond a rickety snow fence that was rough to the touch. I had forgotten both yard and chickens. On a sidewalk outside a city packing house a pre-adolescent memory is struck like a match.

In the window of Oceanic Commercial Inc., importers: a Michael Jackson poster. In the window of Toronto Watch Imports Inc.: two Michael Jackson posters. In the window of Superior Wholesalers: six Michael Jackson buttons, two Michael Jackson key rings, three head-and-shoulders photographs of Michael Jackson, one in an acrylic frame perfect for desk or dresser top. In the window of Ganesh Imports Ltd.: a Michael Jackson poster, a Michael Jackson mirror, four Michael Jackson buttons, a package of pocket-sized address books with Michael Jackson on the cover, two assortments of Michael Jackson key rings (six each), three packages of Michael Jackson stickers, a framed Michael Jackson portrait, and a framed Michael Jackson portrait with – incorporated into the frame – a battery-powered quartz clock. The clock shows 10:05, the right time.

A man comes out of Spadina Textiles carrying bolts of cloth that he arranges on weathered wooden display stands. At Canada Surplus Jobbers another man does the same. At Senior Custom Upholstery, at United Housewares and Gifts, at Trans-European Textiles, clerks carry out armloads of cloth and kitchen implements and stacks of plastic garbage cans, all to be piled along the sidewalk. Spadina is setting up for business.

Outside Vientiane Trading Co. and outside Four Five Six Trading Co. swarms of women with shopping bags pick over piled oranges. The oranges are such a vivid colour that they vibrate in my memory like a clear note that rings long after the orchestra has stopped playing.

Wall of love

Picture this: a wall, seventy-eight, maybe eighty paces long, three storeys high. It looks like your basic concrete block wall, which it is. It is the outside back wall of a sort of a little auto repair plaza on Bloor, out near High Park. Around front there is a Midas Muffler and a Minit-Tune and an Atlas Transmission.

The best view of the wall is from the subway train as it pulls into or leaves the east end of the Keele station. The train travels along a couple of hundred metres of elevated track there and all that is between it and the wall is a parking lot, sort of down below.

Painted on the wall are some of the gaudiest expressions of graffiti love ever sprayed. Constant exposure to these glorious declarations, even subliminally, must mush the hearts of commuters who ride past the wall every day. That would explain why so many subway riders from Keele on west are so charged with affection when they get off downtown that they're busting to hug someone, although they restrain themselves because this is, after all, Toronto and some of them are from Etobicoke and don't want to appear unfamiliar with Toronto ways.

CAUTION: everything written on the wall is not about love. There is a little politics. "No Cruise tests!" "Canada out of NATO!" There is a little rock 'n' roll. "Pink Floyd!" There is a little political rock 'n' roll. "Anarchy or Bust!" And there is the f-word, although it is inconspicuous and is probably there just for form's sake since you can't have an official graffiti wall without it. It is a regulation.

All the rest, though – all the rest is love.

"Sophie I love you," in a florid, flowing, unaffectedly direct style.

"Kevin loves Trish," in a boxy, sturdy script.

A great (!) big (!) red (!) heart pierced by a cupid arrow the size of a cruise missile. Written on the heart, in splendid solitude, "Paula." But, and here we descend through the circles of romance, after the Paula on the heart there is a question mark: "?" What do you imagine might be the question that question mark is asking? What do you imagine the answer was? Ah, sweet mystery of love.

"I love you Chris."

"I love you Tina." Apparently Tina is loved by a swain who goes both ways, since he immediately thereafter wrote, "Tina I love you."

"Sweet Elena."

A "Bren" in big brash letters floating among big brash hearts.

But biggest and brashest of all, an artistic *coup d'éclat* that would make a fitting tattoo for the chest of Michelangelo's David, had David the chest of King Kong: "LORI" in letters of gold, bracketed by huge half hearts, the centre of the "o" is a little red heart, the dot on the "i" is a little red heart, all arrayed against a blue-and-white checkerboard sky. This is bubblegum art in bold strokes.

But the most singular statement of all is the least well drawn. The lover who did it risked much because he climbed to the roof, a dangerous undertaking, and lay as if he were on the edge of a cliff while attempting to manipulate a spray can to paint the face of it, as it stretched sharply down from him, disappearing into the, I imagine, dark. He got the odd letter backward and even missed a couple, which he went back later and squeezed in. But that is all technicals. Forget the technicals. Read what he wrote.

"JANICE – PRECIOUS INFLUENCE: SWEET STRENGTH: LOVING HEART/I LOVE YOU: VINCENT"

Well, now. That's what you have to call something, isn't it? I don't believe Robert Browning and old Elizabeth Barrett had enough guts between them to come up with a statement half as real on what it is that goes on between a guy and his girl. Mind you, I don't know that Robert Browning ever worked with an aerosol paint can, and the medium can have a considerable effect on what you want to get across. I mean, some things just *look* better sprayed on a wall than they do printed on a page.

I don't care about that, though. I just care about *effect*. Can you imagine it?

Can you imagine Vincent pointing it out to Janice as they go whizzing by on the subway?

Her lips start to tremble.

Her breasts start to heave.

"Oh, Vincent!" she cries, melting into his sinewy arms as the train plunges into the station.

Blackout.

Landmarks to go

The press of other business kept me from being present when the world's largest Kentucky Fried Chicken bucket was erected beside the Gardiner Expressway, across from the Canadian National Exhibition, and when I arrived it was *fait accompli.*

With its distinctive red-and-white markings, it bears a likeness of Colonel Harlan Sanders, the late culinary wizard whose original recipe, employing thirteen herbs and spices in secret combination, inspired one of the great fast-food stories, and undoubtedly the greatest fried chicken story, of the era. Beside his face are his celebrated words, "It's finger lickin' good."

Built to the exact proportions of the Kentucky Fried Chicken buckets sold in local outlets, the world's largest one is 83 feet above ground at its base and rises 23 feet to a height of 106 feet. It joins the CN Tower, the Royal York Hotel, and the clustered downtown bank towers as a dominant feature of the city skyline. It will soon outstrip other city delights as a tourist attraction.

Guided tours of the bucket, conducted by well-informed young men and women in appropriate dress (string tie, white shirt, dark slacks, shoes carefully shined), will show how handsomely it rises above the less lofty contributions of mere advertisers to the city's scenic wonders – a good number of which, coincidentally, are concentrated in the very area where the world's largest Kentucky Fried Chicken bucket stands, to catch the attention of travellers on the expressway and the GO trains that rush into and out of the metropolis.

When you examine the great cities of the world you soon learn that each has something outstanding about it that has come to represent it symbolically in the eyes of the world. In Houston it is the Astrodome, in Seattle it's the Kingdome – each in its own way setting it apart from Minneapolis-St. Paul with the Metrodome and Pontiac with the Silverdome. Toronto is domeless. A city without a dome is a poor relation, a hick town. Nobody returns its calls.

Since construction of a dome is in the hands of the provincial government, leading to speculation that it will not likely blot out the light of day before the next ice age arrives, or perhaps even after it departs, the city fathers set out to provide a substitute that might add some allure to their faded gem.

It led to quite a debate. Some councillors favoured erecting a 100-foot-tall white-wine spritzer, since it represented the active, modern approach the city takes and would illustrate how closely attuned it is to the trends that are each generation's signature.

On the other side of the debate – council was split, naturally, right and left – on the conservative side, were those who maintained that what most typified the city were the basic virtues of goodness and decency, home and family. These rallied around a proposal to build the world's largest meatloaf. Plans called for including plumbing and heating equipment to create a steady wisp of steam that would rise from the dark, meaty surface, just the way it used to when Dad arrived home from work and we all sat down at the supper table together.

Compromise – joyous compromise, sensible compromise – was achieved when it was agreed that nobody in his right mind liked white-wine spritzers, and that nobody had seen a home-made meatloaf in so long that most people might not recognize one, certainly not children reared in day care. (And the more they thought about it, anyway, whenever Dad arrived home and there was meatloaf on the table there was a terrible fight during dinner. Usually about money. Those were trying times. Psychiatrists have grown wealthy on what are known in the trade as "meatloaf memories.")

The compromise? When you get right down to it, Toronto basically is a Kentucky Fried Chicken kind of town. Everybody agreed on that.

Curious to know just how high a profile the world's largest Kentucky Fried Chicken bucket had given the city, I called Milton's Downtowner Bar & Grill in Youngstown, New York, and asked if they could see it looming above Lake Ontario's northern horizon. The customer I spoke with said he believed he could, but if I called back during happy hour he'd be able to see it for sure.

Hi, sailor!

Hi there, sailor. New in town? Indeed he is. And like all sailors through seafaring history, the sailors who sail all this weary way have a hankering for some shore leave.

And we do our best to show them a good time. Why, just last year we marched a batch of sailors who came in those little short tall ships up to City Hall where they got to meet the mayor. "Hello, sailors," he said.

It is difficult to imagine a seaman who had spent forty days and forty nights or however long they spend, before the mast or wherever they spend it, who could want for more in the way of a good time than to meet the mayor.

But some might. Some might feel cooped up aboard those little tiny tall ships and care to have what is known as some rest and recreation. They might well want to visit the Royal Ontario Museum.

The museum has, after all, just undergone a major renovation. It boasts world-class collections. It is a major tourist attraction, one that few sailors would want to pass up. The trouble, of course, is that being new in town, they don't know anybody who lives here. How could they find somebody to go to the museum with them?

Not to worry, sailor. If you need a friend during your visit to our city, you need look no further than the Yellow Pages, under E for Escort Service, to find a perfect companion – or companions, since there are nearly twelve pages of them to choose from.

We're an extremely friendly town, sailor.

How about Cherry Blossom Escorts – "Tantalizing & Appetizing"? Cherry Blossom is open for business from noon to one a.m., which should give you plenty of time to fit in a trip to the museum and maybe go somewhere after for a cheeseburger and a chocolate malt.

Or if the museum seems too racy, if you want something a little less sophisticated, what could be more appropriate than a visit to Casa Loma with a friend from Divine Innocence Escorts? How divinely innocent it would be to stroll through the baronial splendor of Sir Henry Pellat's creation – to admire the battlements, to see the ballroom where Glenn Gray and his big band once played. Divine Innocence promises to be "discreet & provocative."

Or if you prefer the outdoors, why not stroll in Edwards Gardens with a tomato from Eve's Garden. Eve's Garden offers to come "discreetly to your door" but a hatch will suffice. If you do have a door, if by chance you've been marooned in a hotel, you might prefer Room Service. Room Service is "divinely decadent."

If the idea of decadence surprises you in Toronto, you should know that this is a proudly cosmopolitan city. Consider that there are French Quarter Executive Escorts "for every mood & every moment" and Lisa's Taste of the Orient, and Cheri – "Limousines provided upon request." Not to mention Danielle Danielle, Desiree, and Finesse. Cheques and major credit cards accepted. "Sometimes you need a little finesse, sometimes you need a lot." And Fantasy Femmes Ltd. will "make your fantasy a reality."

For the pet-loving sailor, there are Friendly Bunnys, Rent-a-Bunnie, Hire a Bunny, and Kitty Galore's Cuddly Companions. If his interest lies more in the realm of fashion, he might try Silk Stockings, Silk and Satin, or Leather and Lace Introductions.

If the weather is bad, he can "Call any day for Rainy Day Services." If the night is dark, there is Moonflower. If the stars are right, try Zodiac. "Match your sign for an entertaining afternoon or evening." And if he's plumb tuckered out and doesn't want to go anywhere, he can call Person to Person for an "intimate, relaxing telephone conversation."

The loyal sailor might care for Her Majesty's Service, while the man who has sailed the seven seas and is far from home will discover that "ladies speak over 5 different languages" at By Invitation Only.

Should he crave intellectual stimulation, Temptation Executive Escort Service offers "a lovely, sensitive and university educated lady to pamper a discriminating gentleman."

And for the little sailor who misses his Mom, how happy he will be with A Little Older . . . A Lot Better. Cookies and cocoa included? Why not?

A sailor could walk his fingers off in Toronto's Yellow Pages.

Glorious slush

As I walked out the other day, it occurred to me that no one has ever celebrated slush.

Mud has its laureates. "Mud, mud, glorious mud, there's nothing quite like it for cooling the blood – " is the song the hippopotamuses sing as you slide along the Nile in your caique, if that is what you slide along the Nile in.

But "Slush, slush, glorious slush, there's nothing quite like it for – " what? See? Why of Nature's creations is slush, almost alone, unsung? Even rocks and gravel got their innings. Somebody was always whaling away at them with a nine-pound hammer and shouting Lordy, Lordy.

Snow is everybody's darling. How many times people have built a snowman and pretended it was Parson Brown I can't begin to tell you. A lot. People go sliding down snowy hills shouting Hosannas. People admire the intricate artistry that creates the delicate star-shaped snowflake – each one unique. People try to catch snowflakes on the tips of their tongues and turn around three times before it melts because they know it is a guaranteed way to get a wish to come true. People don't get off on slush like that at all. Mostly when people see a lot of slush they get gloomy and slash their wrists, or the wrists of loved ones.

Look at icebergs. Somebody has just written an entire book about an iceberg – the one that sank the Titanic. *It gives the iceberg's version of the events. Nobody ever bothered to ask slush for its side of the story. The minute you look at an iceberg a voice tells you, "That's just the tip of the iceberg. Nine-tenths of it is beneath the surface." Very heavy symbolism. A voice never tells you anything when you look at slush. What is there to tell? What you see is what you get.*

For raw glamour, consider glaciers. Expeditions set off to cross glaciers. It can take weeks. Sometimes they disappear into crevasses. If anybody took it in mind to glamourize slush, it would help to have an expedition or two disappear in it. There's nothing like the dis-appearance of an expedition to raise your standing with the public. The public will accept nothing less these days.

The public is also keen to learn that a village has been wiped out by some natural phenomenon, like say a landslide, or a mudslide, or a rockslide, or a snowslide. Give the public pictures of gallant rescue workers sticking long poles down into the debris of an avalanche as they try to find survivors of the village that has been wiped out and they'll come running back for more.

Whoever heard of a slushslide?

Just to demonstrate what a low opinion everybody has of slush, look where they put it in the dictionary. Just after "slurp" and "slurry" and just before "slut." That's not a neighbourhood where a decent word would want to be seen. It's a bad-news part of town. If we want to reclaim slush, one thing we might do is move it out of there and put it up with "financier" or "curtsey," some place where it might have half a chance to make something of itself.

There are slush funds. High rollers throw a few bucks into slush funds to bribe officials. (Nobody ever bribes unofficials. Remember that. Some day it will come in handy.) Strange it should be called "slush fund." A mud fund would be more appropriate. But no, mud has friends in high places. Poor slush, it might already be beyond salvation.

Those of us who live in Toronto have to admit, if we're being honest – really honest, honest-to-goodness gosh-darned honest, cross-our-hearts-and-hope-to-die honest – which we sometimes aren't, being occasionally given to self-deception, that the outstanding feature of winter in this sloppy metropolis is slush.

The thing that distinguishes Torontonians from their fellow Canadians between the months of November and April is wet feet. Soakers. Cold feet, sure, and all that connotes if connotes is what it does. But wet feet, clammy feet all wrinkled and mouldy and shrivelled up like blue prunes. That's us.

We must like it because the minute there's not enough slush, we call out the salt trucks to make more.

As I said, I walked out in the slush the other day and my feet got soaking wet, so I went back home and wrote this. That's how it happened.

8
Write-Offs

My first novel

Forty years ago Graham Greene wrote a novel, *The Tenth Man*, that was never published. In the intervening years he completely forgot about it.

Recently the manuscript was found and forwarded to Greene, who read it and decided it was pretty good. It has just been published.

That can happen easily enough – forgetting you wrote something. Being a writer, I know that I often forget stuff I have written. Sometimes I get to the bottom of a page and can't for the life of me remember what it was I wrote at the top. Often I will go back and see if the last sentence I wrote is in any way related to the sentence I am currently writing, but sometimes when you're in a rush to meet a deadline you don't have time, so you just soldier on and hope for the best. There's no room in writing for the timid.

Now that this has happened to Graham Greene – finding an entire novel he had forgotten writing – it has got me thinking. It wouldn't surprise me in the least if I have written a novel and it has slipped my mind. Because it certainly has slipped my mind. I can't remember a thing about it. I can't even remember if I wrote it yesterday or twenty years ago. If somebody comes up to me and says, "Hey, we found this novel you wrote," I'll feel exactly the way Greene felt. Who? Me? What? A novel? You're kidding!

It could easily be a masterpiece of Canadian literature. It doesn't take all that much to produce a Canadian literary masterpiece. It has to contain a lot of moaning about geography – I don't mean about the subject, Geography, you took in school; I mean about rocky coasts and dustblown prairies and things of that nature – and it has to devote a lot of time and energy to descriptions of weather (lousy)

144

and it has to run about 400 pages, because what people want in a literary masterpiece is the feeling they got their money's worth.

I don't know whether it will contain the obligatory sex scene – it all depends. If it is an early novel, it most likely won't because I was pretty shy about those things and besides, what if your mother read something you wrote that was dirty? If it's a later work, it probably will, for the practical reason that if you want to sell movie rights you're just about obliged to have an obligatory sex scene or two. What remains to be seen is how many, and how graphic, and, I guess, whether there's any weirdness.

Of course, it might not be a masterpiece. It might be a minor work that, if it should turn up somewhere, and if it should get published, would spend no more than a few weeks on the best-seller lists. Maybe it will be a heart-warming account of growing up in Ontario, a glowing portrait of a boy's quest to become tall. That sounds fairly interesting, doesn't it? And in a novel like that you can get by with just a little heavy petting.

I have no idea where a novel I forget writing might be. It's infuriating, after all that effort put into writing one. I've gone through every drawer in the house and I've started on the boxes in the cellar. God, you can't believe the boxes in the cellar! I even looked in all the suitcases because maybe I took it on a trip and forgot to unpack it. I hope it didn't get sold in the garage sale. We sold a lot of stuff in the garage sale: rickety old chests of drawers, ratty armchairs. Maybe the manuscript was in one of them – you know how things get scrunched in behind drawers or fall down the back of seat cushions. If any of you bought any of that junk, would you kind of scrounge around and see if my novel's in it?

I'll be quite excited to get it because it will be my first – my long-awaited first novel. Of course, since I already managed to forget writing it, I won't be too concerned about what the critics have to say. I'll be able to remain aloof. Besides, that's so Canadian isn't it – the critics dumping, dumping, dumping all the time and never saying a single positive thing about what we produce in this country? But what can you expect from the weaselly types they hire to review books in the first place? Anyway, as I said, I don't care.

Sex and scandal

The neighbourhood ratepayers' association voted a big vote of sympathy to Mila Mulroney, the nation's first lady, after she was down in Palm Springs and told Dinah Shore and some other ladies that thanks to the media her family has lost "the traditional protection of the privacy of . . . home and family."

Mila gave as an example how she never even got a chance to tell her friends about her pregnancy, which was "announced in the press before Brian and I told anyone," the Brian in question being her husband.

Edna Elliot, forty-seven, who lives at No. 42 and who moved the vote of sympathy said, "And how." She had personal experience of how the traditional protection of the privacy of home and family had vanished when the last two times she – Edna – got pregnant it was announced in the press before even she knew about it.

"It wasn't written up as if it was foretold by Jeanne Dixon or nothing of the sort," she said. "It was as bold as could be in black and white. 'Seventh in wind for E. Elliot', and likewise, 'Elliots soon to expect No. 8'." She said she didn't know how the press got the scoops unless they noticed some sort of glint or something in her husband Alfred's eye when he left the Railside after having a few beers on his way home from work.

"Those reporters are everywhere looking for tidbits," said Frances McNeely, forty-one, who lives in the upper duplex across from the bus stop. She wondered if there wasn't some way they could be restricted from the traditional venues of home and family, which drew a sharp riposte from Leo Gorman, eighteen, the ace reporter from the *Ward Weekly*. He said once you started limiting freedom of the press, the next thing you knew you would end up with the sort of feudalism they had in Germany that led to the war.

He said he was for "freedom with responsibility," and cited the example of how, when Frances McNeely started holding daily press conferences to announce her upcoming supper menu, he just reported the facts and refrained from commentary on how "there was a lot of variation on the macaroni theme," and neither did he throw in anything about the general run of her place, which wasn't exactly so neat you could hear a pin drop.

Frances said that just showed what the public was up against when even an ace reporter didn't know the difference between deep background for a menu briefing and a wide-open investigation into a person's housekeeping and personal hygiene with all the stops pulled out. Leo said he thought Frances was attempting to manipulate the media and she should watch out in case it blew up in her face when the tide of public opinion turned against her.

Henry Sturdevant said we should all take a leaf from Mila Mulroney's book where she says she cannot complain since she volunteered for the first lady's job and accepted "the terms and conditions that go with it."

Henry, fifty-three, said he volunteered to live where he lives beside the school and so accepted it when the lifestyle section of the school paper, the *Jr. High Lo-Down*, wrote up how his wife, Denise, forty-six, had left him for Allan Grimley, twenty-three, the mechanic at Shulbert's Esso just after Allan bought the black Trans-Am.

The story had made a big thing about how these separations are hardest on the children, which according to Leo Gorman's "Media Watch" column in the *Ward Weekly* was stretching things a bit since the Sturdevants' only child, Richard, twenty-seven, was in jail at the time of the split and had been long before Allan Grimley ever came to work at Shulbert's.

Evaleen Johnson, thirty-eight, said a person with nothing to hide has no need to fear the media as she obviously didn't since she invited the neighbourhood television station, Cable 15, to actually move into her house and do all their broadcasting from there. No matter what show is on, there's Evaleen in the background drinking coffee or fixing her hair or talking on the phone.

Sometimes if there's no show on, they just leave the camera running and Evaleen talks into it about her life and what she intends to do the next day and how she's saving for a vacation down south. Evaleen, who lives alone, had Henry Sturdevant over for supper the other night and ratings zoomed, but nothing came of it.

Grammar, safe and easy

Being slight of build, with muscles like rose petals, I was never much of a hand at grammar. To hew a sentence out of raw words called for heft. You had to be able to take grammar in both hands like a club and beat the words until they were all smoothed out in a straight line that began where you were standing and ended up somewhere in the vicinity of where you wanted to get to.

You were obliged to wear steel-toed boots when you whaled away with grammar, and safety glasses in case a gerund flew up and lodged in your eye. The compensation board had cases lined out the door of writers who had strained something or pulled something when a compound sentence broke loose and they tried to wrestle it back on to the page.

There were technical advances, but even with the pneumatic grammar you had to be built like a draught horse to get much use out of it. A scrawny person attempting to use it could jounce himself silly without coming up with much of anything that wasn't full of lumps. Besides, the racket was so terrible that it was impossible to concentrate on what you were writing, and it drove the neighbours nuts.

Nowadays, of course, there is the word processor, and there's no longer any need to know how to wield grammar. It's been automated. Stuff a load of words in the hopper, throw a lever, leave it to grind for a few seconds, and out she comes, prose smooth as peanut butter.

The Ministry of Education has discovered that schoolchildren today can be as fresh as daisies after turning out not just sentences, but entire paragraphs that would have ground their grandparents into dust, and it's all because of the word processor. While this is swell, and we have all these junior whiz-bangs who can churn out stuff that reads as sweet as the breeze on a summer afternoon, it's not as swell as you might think because while they can write all right they can't seem to produce anything profound.

They lack, according to the ministry, the ability to compose effective written arguments. "They don't appear to have a sense of what an argument should look like." Whenever they fuel up the word processor and turn it on, the muse takes whatever it is they had hoped would come out, wrings it out like a dishrag, and turns it into "invented narrative," of which these youngsters are considered to have a command that is "often masterly."

That's okay if you intend to write about the Snopes family in Yoknapatawpha County as, for instance, William Faulkner apparently intended to do. But if you hoped to write about why our country should pull on its hip-boots and wade into free trade with the United States, and what came out was the life of the Snopeses, you'll appreciate the sort of problem that our schoolchildren have.

It can happen to the best of us. I set out today to explain, in terms lucid and with reasoning of the highest quality, just why it is that free trade will either be the jim-dandiest thing that ever happened to every man-jack of us, or it won't, but the word processor got stricken with the theme of grammar and took off on its own. All I've been able to do is hang on for dear life and hope it eventually runs out of steam.

The people from the ministry say one reason the students don't know how to lay an argument out is because "They probably don't read editorials in the newspapers." If that's true, it's hard to believe they ever make it through the day. Editorials in newspapers don't just show you how to construct a shapely argument, they tell you when your roof needs new shingles, how long to boil the broccoli, whether to indulge in free trade, and everything else you ever need to know about everything.

They also make good poultices for boils; are useful as insulation, being airtight by nature; and doctors who don't like to use gas on their patients have them read an editorial before surgery, although this is done sparingly because a patient who reads too many of them will slip into a coma.

What the ministry didn't know is that editorial writers are equipped with argument processors. These have three settings: "High time," "View with alarm," and "Government waste."

Argument processors will soon be available to schoolchildren, and then everything will be fine. Also more clearer.

How to write

This is being written in a great rush because I have to get out of here and go talk to journalism students about being a journalist. One thing I can tell them is that you'll never be much of a journalist if you always write in a great rush. The other thing I can tell them is that being a journalist you'll never get rich. And that's about it. It will be a short talk.

But that's all right. Then the students can get out of the classroom early and drink beer or make love or read Mark Twain's *Life on the Mississippi* or get on with their nervous breakdowns or do anything else under God's green sky that reminds them that living is living and that journalism – well, that journalism isn't the kissing, it's only the telling.

That said, if journalism is still what they care to do, they might as well do it well. So I will pass on some useful tricks.

By doing the following, anybody can improve anything they write

100 per cent – whether it's a letter, a club report, a shopping list, a memorandum, the lead editorial in *The Star*, the great Canadian novel, or *The Last Spike* by Pierre Berton. Anything. I guarantee it. You won't believe it can be so simple.

1. Learn to read all over again. Learn to read for technique. When Mark Twain describes thunder, how does he make it sound like thunder? How does Woody Allen make us laugh? What sort of detail does Jane Austen give us to make Emma sound too precious by half?

2. Practise. Nobody practises writing. Everybody thinks, "I speak the language, I should be able to write it." I can hum a tune, but would I sit at the Steinway at a concert in Massey Hall without practising hours a day for years? Nope. So why should I expect to come cold to a sheet of paper and whip off something lyrical and moving? I shouldn't expect to. It is hard work, writing.

3. Rewrite. Don't ever show anybody the first draft of anything. A second draft is always better. A third better still.

4. Read your stuff out loud to yourself. In your mind you always know what you intended to say and how you intended to say it. Your eye is accustomed to feeding written stuff to your mind. They are like an old married couple who can leave a lot out and still know what the other is talking about. But you write most times for other people, often strangers, who don't know your codes and shorthand, who aren't insiders like your mind and eye. Let your ear be editor.

When you read aloud, your ear will tell you, "That phrase sounds awkward," "I've lost track of what this sentence is about," "People don't talk like this," "This rhythm is herky-jerky." Your ear can be more objective than your eye. If you feel silly reading out loud, lock yourself in the bathroom and do it there.

5. This one is the most fun, and the most amazing. It is called "letting your subconscious do the writing for you and saving yourself a lot of work." I stumbled on it by trial and error, mostly by error. I later read a number of accounts of scientific discoveries and discovered it to be a real and useful and respectable method. It is all laid out in an essay by Isaac Asimov called "The Eureka Phenomenon." All you have to do is concentrate intensely on the material you want to write about, then go away and think about something else for a while and then come back and watch your stuff spin out of your typewriter like gold from straw.

"Eureka," of course, refers to Archimedes saying, "I can't figure this out," and going and having a bath. Asimov: "If you let go, then the thinking process comes under automatic involuntary control and is more apt to take new pathways and make erratic associations you would not think of consciously. The solution will then come while you *think* you are *not* thinking. . . . I suspect that voluntary thought may possibly prepare the ground (if even that), but that the final touch, the real inspiration, comes when thinking is under involuntary control."

Asimov likes a mindless action movie to switch his mind from the subject at hand. I get a cup of tea, read the sports pages.

6. Keep it short.

There. Now you know everything I know. When I finish with the students, I will go for a walk, maybe drink beer, maybe make love.

The $1.5 million write-off

I have got a rubber chicken. Last week, some of you may remember, I wrote that I had fleas. You will be thinking, "That Slinger has always got something." I'll tell you this, there's a world of difference between having a rubber chicken and having fleas.

You will be thinking, "Big deal. Who cares what the difference is? All I know is I never know when I might look in this part of the paper and read something that gives me the hoobada-hoobadas."

Listen, it is a small price to pay. Look at it this way: when you read here, you never have to send one eye scouting ahead to make sure you are not going to read about any problems associated with feminine ailments, you know what I mean?

That has got to ease your mind a fair whack right off the bat. But how many times have you ever given me credit for that? How many times have you ever got to the end of one of these columns and said, "Whew! Not one single word about feminine ailments, you know what I mean? Slinger has done it again." Not even once, that's how many times you've done it.

But I mention some little things that are bothering me, such as these fleas I've got or this rubber chicken, figuring there should be some *quid pro quo* between us, expecting maybe the slightest bit of sympathy, and what happens? Listen, if it gives you the squeams, what I recommend is you boil the newspaper before reading any further. Sterilize the sucker. A lot of people do it as a matter of course. It's a big world. A lot of things are going around. You never can tell what might make it through and get you.

You don't have to tell me what a risk it is reading these days. It's a bigger risk writing, believe me. You see some of this stuff in its raw state and the hoobada-hoobadas are a mild reaction. The only reason I put up with it is for the money. The money is extremely good, let me tell you. I get maybe $1.5 million a year for doing this. That's not too shabby is it? A person can put up with a fair bit of raw data direct from the real world for that kind of mazoola.

Actually, most of that money comes in overtime. My basic weekly is – wait, I got a stub here – yeah, it's $121.50. Times fifty-two. So that's roughly, oh, $1,494,683 in overtime. Per year, mind you. But then I am never off duty. My mind is working all the time, even when I sleep. Even when I brush my teeth. Even when I watch television. The old mind never stops. That's sixteen and a half hours a day overtime, plus weekends, plus statutory holidays. It adds up.

You maybe didn't know that. You maybe thought this was cheap-ola, soup-label writing such as you're used to reading elsewhere in the paper. I admit it has many surface similarities in spelling and punctuation and even in vocabulary, since the computer only permits the use of 350 approved words. These words are taken out and examined by the proprietor once a year to see how they have held up.

Occasionally a new one gets added. This year, for example, "climax" was added, presumably because it might lend a nice touch to descriptions of the conclusions of sporting contests and plays and movies and such. Unfortunately it led to a roaring torrent of stories associated with feminine ailments, you know what I mean? Which, at least, you have been protected from in this space. I have seen to that.

No. The writing you get here is quality stuff, top-of-the-line. That is because it is about a real life, an actual real life that is lived twenty-four hours a day, even while watching television. You get the full treatment, the hopes, the fears, the dreams, the aspirations. The whole schmear. The blood, the guts, the spleen, the intestines, the hair follicles, the thing on my toe. Nothing is held back in this kind of first-class writing because otherwise it wouldn't have vitality, it wouldn't pulsate, or throb, or go squish when you step on it in the dark in your bare feet.

So *that's* why I told you about the fleas, and it's why I'm going to tell you about the rubber chicken. Because I don't stint. I don't cheat you. I give honest weight. You can count on it every time.

This rubber chicken was different than anything I had ever got before. It led me to examine my life.

Upper Volta gets a jolt

An esteemed fellow columnist, Zena Cherry, once reported on a splashy freeload given in aid of Upper Volta. At the conclusion of her report she wrote one of the most delightful and succinct sentences in the history of journalism. After listing the more prominent guests she spent some time describing the country (a sorry state in a sorry state, or words to that effect) and then wrapped it all up thus:

"There is no Lower Volta."

The idea of an upper with no lower always struck me as an exquisite assymetry, something foreign to nature (e.g., Upper and Lower Canada, Silesia, east side, berths, dentures, classes, etc.). It was geopolitical slapstick, the equivalent of waiting for the other shoe to fall and . . . it never did.

Now there is no Upper Volta either.

The current new regime celebrated its first anniversary in power by changing the name of the country to Bourkina Fasso, which translates as "Country of Incorruptible Men," as fine and idealistic a name for a country as you are likely to run across, and an optimistic one as well, considering that Saye Zerbo, the former president, is serving fifteen years for corruption.

Now the country is clean as a whistle, new sense of purpose, new determination to feed its starving population, new resolve to eliminate all traces of petty bourgeois ideology (the petty bourgeois line is usually drawn at LaCoste shirts). And all it took was a new name.

Statecraft is simple once you get the hang of it. It works like that old joke about being a creature from outer space. You point your finger at somebody and say, "Zap, you're sterile."

Individuals should be so smart. Richard Nixon is getting a nice new image as a wise and trusted Republican thinker, but there's no way he can assume a public role because too many people will think back and say, "Hey, it's that rat Nixon again. No way." If he changed his name to, say, Roosevelt Yellowbird, then people could ignore the past and he'd probably pick up a good whack of black and native Indian votes in the bargain.

At least Bourkina Fasso kept the name of the old capital, Ouagadougou. It is a great African name; I doubt that Edgar Rice Burroughs could have come up with a better one. It has what I imagine to be an African beat. If it was the last beat Mr. Kurtz heard from the Heart of Darkness it would have been wholly appropriate. Sometimes when you get into a writing frame of mind and you come to Ouagadougou you don't want to stop. Ouagadougoudougoudougoudou-goudougou.

Anyway, there doesn't seem to be any doubt that Ouagadougou is African. With Upper Volta you were never sure. Maybe because it sounds like Volga. I always thought it should be in Russia, somewhere near the Ukraine. Think how it would have been, the Red Cossacks fighting the White Cossacks and suddenly, flying across the steppe, comes a whole bunch of guys dressed in Ostrich plumes waving spears and beating on their shields.

One cossack turns to another cossack and says, "Who are those guys?"

"They're the cossacks from Upper Volta, tovarich. The Black Cossacks."

"Yikes!"

I realize that, by and large, the world is a more fevered place than it appears to be to someone sitting on, say, my balcony, drinking, say, gin. Things don't stay still for long. There was a time in school when I had the map of Africa off by heart. Since then it has been shuffled and reshuffled and become, for me, terra incognita. Goodnight, Dr. Livingstone, wherever you are.

Listen, good luck to you, Bourkina Fasso. It is a great idea having a country that is inhabited by none but the incorrupt. I'm surprised it took so long for somebody to come up with it. Canadians are always full of good intentions; we might be the next to follow suit.

I, however, am appropriating the name Upper Volta for my own country. As king of Upper Volta I will wear a triangular hat folded out of newspapers, much like the one Christopher Robin wore. And I will carry a sword nailed together out of slats. As king, I will invite Zena Cherry to sit on my balcony and drink gin. We will discuss worldly affairs. She will write, "There is no Lower Volta."

Call our toll-free numbers

Hey, hey, hello! Here we are smack in the middle of our fund-raising campaign but before we get down to business we just want to say how glad we are that you could take a few minutes out of your busy, busy schedules to be with us. You know, on a personal level, day in, day out, year in, year out, as we bring you this material, we keep coming back to that old saying in our business. Without you out there, there wouldn't be us in here. So, from the heart, thanks.

Our phone lines are manned and waiting for your calls and soon we'll talk with the volunteer who is manning those lines. If you're within our reading area, the number to call is 555-8778. If you're outside our reading area, call our toll-free number, 1-800-5598.

And if you're not now reading this and don't plan to, write to us here care of this column and we'll send you a brochure on how you, too, can make your dollars count in the information age.

Remember, this is not a charity. This is not publicly funded journalism. This is a profit-making venture in the marketplace of ideas and depends entirely on cash flow to keep going. Notice that there is no advertising in this space. In order to fund advertising-free space like this we depend entirely on contributions from you, our readers, and our phone lines are open.

We are especially pleased to be able to offer valuable premiums, premiums that you will enjoy and that will remind you of your personal contribution. Right now, if you pledge $10 you can clip this column from the newspaper and stick it on the front of your fridge.

For pledges of $730 we make this one-time offer: a whole dump-truck-load of French fries will be dumped on your front lawn; think of the good times you'll have with all those French fries, not to mention the savings. And for anonymous gifts of $5,000 or more we will arrange to have a long-lost relative flown to this country to live with you.

Here again are those numbers. If you're in our reading area but can't read, 555-8778, or, of you can read but have fallen down in a ditch somewhere and nobody can hear your cries for help, phone toll-free 1-800-5598.

Here are some of the things we hope to be offering in upcoming editions thanks to your generosity.

A brand new supply of adjectives; we plan to replace our tired, old adjectives with superlatives, tiredest, oldest, fastest, mostest – these are just a few that we'll be bringing you.

Truth is high on our list, but truth doesn't come cheap. Without your support we'll be forced to rely on half-truths, rumour, innuendo, and, frequently, outright lies, which are all we can afford in these times of budgetary restraint. Won't you support truth in journalism?

And implementation of a non-discriminatory, full-alphabet quota policy. If we can meet our fund-raising objective of $6 million we will endeavour to establish a non-discriminatory quota system to ensure that each letter of the alphabet receives equal use in every column.

Remember, when you call you don't have to send the cash right away. All you're making is a pledge and, once you make it, interest on your pledge will increase by only 6 per cent a day until you finally send it in, which should certainly provide an incentive. Or, if a single lump sum is more than you can manage, we have a convenient payroll-deduction scheme: you tell us which bank your payroll is deposited in and we'll send armed representatives around to deduct it.

The numbers to remember are 555-8778 if you know what's good for you and 1-800-5598 toll-free if you have left the country and are living under an assumed name. Here is our volunteer, now. Say a few words, Mom. "Hi. I think this is just a wonderful way to improve the quality of material in this space, especially for people who don't want to get their cars blown up."

Thanks, Mom. Now, I see some of our lines are clear. You know, some people think that what we do is just a job. But to us it's a lot more than that. To us it's a chance to make $6 million, and none of us can think of anything that we would care to do that compares even slightly. That's why we love it so much and that's why we love you.

Here are the numbers to call.

Gun news, balloon news

Gun news dominates the papers and the broadcast reports these days. Quebec provides a lot of gun news. Gunmen prowl the National Assembly, spraying machine gun bullets into anybody who's handy. Sleeping carpetlayers are quelled by shots fired through the doors of small-town motels.

Gun news follows the Pope. Either real guns or fake ones, it doesn't much matter. Ireland, El Salvador, the Levant. Some days there's so much gun news it won't all fit, it overflows across the floor and has to be mopped up by the newsroom cleaners.

It's hard to imagine what they did for news before they had gun news. It's like trying to imagine what we breathed before there was air.

I went back to the files to find out, went through the brittle, fading clippings, through the brittle, fading microfilm of that forgotten era. I found the press back then was full of balloon news.

Here was a banner headline: "Blue Balloon Seen In Square." Under it was a smaller heading: "Noon-hour crowds witness stray balloon." There followed a detailed account of the incident, including quotations from eyewitnesses. "A balloon? Sure I saw it. It was right over there." And "Yep, it was quite a sight."

From abroad the wire services supplied balloon dispatches. One told of a balloon merchant in Paris who sold balloons on sticks. From Berlin came a report of balloons that had things written on them. "Happy Birthday." "Thinking of you." Things like that. Only in German.

There was a letter to the editor from a man who said that in his youth his father had given him a balloon filled with helium. He had kept it, hoping to leave it to his own children. But one day he opened the box he stored it in and the balloon popped out. A breeze flipped it out the door and down the hall and out of the house.

The man said he chased after the balloon. "I ran like anything, but it was no use." Outside it rose quickly. Soon it was above the roof. Soon it was above the trees. Soon it was way up in the sky. "I watched it go up and up," wrote the man. "It became a dot, then it became less than a dot, then I couldn't see it any more. Now I don't know what I'll leave my children."

When I turn on the news or read the paper it seems that no broadcast or edition is complete without the latest rundown on babies that died tragically. It has been this way for as long as I care to remember. Finding it in the news makes us sad and we wonder how the world became such a terrible place.

What was the world like before it became such a terrible place? What was in the news before babies started dying and judges and lawyers picked through the circumstances and the whole town knew something awful had happened, but it didn't know what?

News about skipping was big. The papers had teams of reporters and photographers who smoked cigarettes and drank countless cups of coffee as they waited for somebody to call in with a skipping tip. Then they rushed out with their ties streaming back over their shoulders. They hurried to the scene in high-powered automobiles.

They called in breathless reports. "Double-dutch seen in school-yards." "More Metro children doing pepper than ever before." In an exclusive interview with *The Star*, a little girl, skipping, said, "I had a little sportscar, two-forty-eight, went around the corner, slammed on the brakes; policeman caught me and put me in jail; how many bottles of ginger ale? One, two, three. . ." right on all the way up to a million.

Sometimes I think that if it wasn't for unemployment and climbing interest rates and economic downturns, you could print the whole paper on a subway transfer. Without all our economic woes there wouldn't be enough news to put at either end of a commercial.

Away back when, before prosperity slipped around the corner and hid, those were the days to be in the news business. Those were the days when the only news was what shape the clouds were. "Cow-shaped clouds seen north of the city," was what the readers got. "Dolphins," reported a housewife. "Clouds like dolphins, every-where."

Not that anyone read the paper in those days. There was nothing in it they needed to know.

The flower bomb

If things are out of whack it is because the forsythia has gone off like a bomb. The first couple of days this week, the flowers were closed. Forsythia about to bloom is like an atom about to be split, it repre-sents an unspeakable amount of potential energy. An Einstein could work out the formula.

These last couple of warm days triggered it – yellow bursts in hedges, by front doorsteps, under bay windows, in the corners of backyard fences. Who can calculate the damage it has done? There isn't a sensibility left intact for miles in any direction.

A man with the excellent name of William Least Heat Moon – he is mainly an Osage Indian – has written a book called Blue Highways. *It is an account of a journey he undertook on the back roads of the United States, the roads coloured blue on the maps. It is an excellent, easy-going book.*

Along the road a ways he was looking over his notes of the trip, the fragments of conversations, the ideas and images he'd taken down. "I hunted a structure in the events," he said, "but randomness was the rule." Later he remembered a tactic he'd been taught during night manoeuvres in the Navy. "To see in deep darkness you don't look directly at an object – you look to the left; you look at something else to see what you really want to see."

That is a provocative thing to think about if you happen to be a consumer of the media, or a perpetrator of it, for that matter. The media are sometimes inclined to stare so directly at things that substance seems to dissolve – the way a word stared at long enough eventually loses all meaning, becomes absurd.

Most creatures cannot abide a direct gaze; for all but the most domestic a stare is an act of aggression, antagonistic. There is a special discomfort we feel when a stranger stares directly at us on the subway or in the supermarket. There is almost a tangible challenge in such a look. And the feeling of privacy being invaded, even in so public a place, is profound.

When we're stared at too directly our best qualities can disappear, as if the soft-focus lens were whipped away and all the blackheads on our nose suddenly appeared in Panavision. In one of his books, Raymond Chandler has Philip Marlowe, the private eye, eyeball some blonde from about thirty feet. She looked sensational. "But up close," mourns Marlowe, "she looked like she was made up to be looked at from thirty feet away."

In journalism it is with pride that we say we have described someone warts and all. This is supposed to mean we have taken a balanced look. But it is not difficult to look so hard at something, to get so close up that, as has been said, all you see is wart. This extreme is no better than the other extreme when it comes to helping us find a little order in a random universe.

Robert Bateman, the wildlife artist, has done a marvellous painting of a coyote in a lordly pose on a rocky rise. In a clump of brush at the foot of the rise, some feet from the coyote, lies an empty Budweiser can – you have to look closely to see it, but once you see it you can no longer not see it. Once you see the flaw in the setting, even off to the side as it is, the emotional focus of the whole painting is changed.

That is why governments and corporations invest so much effort and money in creating and maintaining glossy images. A government probably gets a higher return from appearing efficient than it does from passing worthy laws. You might have a hard time recalling a law the provincial government has passed in the last six months. But you're sure it's been doing something. Why are you so sure? Because of its image.

Love affairs seldom tolerate much close scrutiny. A lover's gaze is enhanced by candlelight. If we look too hard at love we start to see

159

underpinnings, props, facades that might be there simply because love made it worthwhile to put them there. They can look artificial, unpretty, when examined on their own, when taken out of context. Love that demands too many answers isn't love, it's accounting.

The forsythia is a glory, a blast of colour. It delights us. Up close the individual flower is scrawny, unremarkable.

9
Personals

Breaking the forty barrier

An odd thing happened to me. I didn't think it was odd, but from the reactions of people I know it appears to be the oddest thing they can imagine. What happened was I turned forty. I thought turning forty was something that happened to just about everybody, sooner or later. Apparently not. Apparently nobody ever turned forty before.

When people discover I've done it, they treat me as if there was something about me a shade unsettling. They get that look in their eyes that the folks got when Jesus ordered the stone rolled back and Lazarus strolled out bound hand and foot with gravecloths, and with a napkin tied over his face. They're not quite sure whether they should run off somewhere and throw up or rejoice at the sight.

"Well, golly," they say, "how are you?"

And, "How do you feel?"

And, "You're all right, eh? I mean, you're doing all right?"

If you tell them everything's fine, they're disappointed. Teilhard de Chardin said a man who returns from a journey and hasn't been changed by it might as well not have bothered going on the journey. So you're letting them down by not showing at least a small sign that you have been marked by forty years' hard travelling.

I'm misleading you if I say there haven't been any changes. There just haven't been any dramatic changes. They have been more along the lines of tedious changes. For example:

– Sex. Let's start with the biggie. When I turned forty I lost all interest in sex. All interest. Every drop. Instead of sex I am only interested in wearing cardigan sweaters and not sitting in a draught.

Say I'm out with the guys and the subject of sex comes up, as it does sometimes when you're out with the guys. One guy, he says he did this, and the next guy says he did that, and the next guy says he did both this and that and everybody whistles and slaps their knees and says, "Go on!"

Then it gets around to me and I say, "Is it just me or does anybody else get the feeling there's a window open around here someplace?"

– Rest. When I turned forty I started to need a lot of rest. This is not easy to get. Sometimes the very act of getting up in the morning tires me out so much I have to crawl back in bed for a rest. When I'm in bed, though, I no longer sleep for more than an hour or two at a stretch, so being in bed doesn't give me the rest I got into bed to get. Resting tires me out.

– Vision. Strangely, my vision improved. That little box on the pay slip where they make the pension plan contributions – I never saw that until I turned forty.

– Politics. It's not that after I turned forty I suddenly took an interest in politics. But when I turned forty I started to believe that it mattered who the leader of the Progressive Conservative Party was.

– Food. Soft food is all I can handle. Yoghurt is good. Cottage cheese. Jell-O. Arrowroot cookies soften up nicely if I dip them in my tea. Steak is all right and so is chicken if I've got lots of time to cut it up into little tiny chunks and then moosh it around before putting it in my mouth. And baby food spread on toast – after a while I got used to it and it's not too bad at all. Nourishing. Easy to fix.

– Wardrobe. When I turned forty I felt an urge to wear neckties with my sports shirts, especially with my plaid sports shirts. Also, I started to hike my trousers way up and buckle them over the top of my tummy, instead of low and lean on my hips. Also cardigan sweaters (see above).

– Friendship. When I turned forty I noticed that my friends didn't invite me over for supper as much as they might. And when they did, all they wanted to talk about was themselves. I decided I'm not that crazy about my old friends and so I'm in the market for some new ones, preferably wealthier and not so tight-fisted.

– I.Q. It dropped about a point an hour after forty. People realize this and they help out by talking to me slower, and louder.

A mug's game

I got out of the gate ahead of the Baby Boom. I missed out on being a beatnik. I missed being a hippie. I missed being a yippie. My generation wasn't lost, it was misplaced. Naturally, I missed being a yuppie. Just when the Young Urban Professionals are throwing their weight around in elections and getting on the covers of newsmagazines, just when yuppies have come into flower, I have gone to seed.

I am a Middle-aged Urban Guy, a mug. That's all. A mass movement with very little mass in any of the right places any more and no movement at all when it can be avoided. Mugs are not a statistically significant group. There is no consensus among mugs. We come in editions of one and like it that way. There is one here and one there and another one over there. I am the one here. This is a report on the phenomenon.

I am 5 feet, 8½ inches tall, except when I slouch, which I do more and more. I have a pecuniary interest in a house that needs work, two cars in varying degrees of repair, a wife in a similar state, a stepdaughter, a stepson, and a dog, all of an independent turn of mind, generally contrary. We get along better than the Great Powers, but we have moments when a little strategic arms limitation talking is in order. It always surprises me to encounter someone so short-sighted as to be unable to see in me one of the most reasonable and easy-going of men.

I have quit jogging, I hope for the last time. My golf game is lousy and getting worse. I wear glasses, but don't need them yet to read. My six upper front choppers were recently installed and are scarcely broken in. My hair is thin, but not thinning, if you know what I mean. It is an important distinction. My bladder is the size of a walnut and keeps me hopping, especially since I drink a lot of beer. It doesn't matter what kind, it all tastes the same.

I smoke du Maurier cigarettes and am at my most boring on the subject of quitting, which I have tried to do so many times it bores me to think about it. It has been years since I smoked marijuana. It made me paranoid. I don't need marijuana to get paranoid. Smoking marijuana to get paranoid was gilding the lily. I have tried cocaine and haven't the least urge to try it again. I have voted Conservative and haven't the least urge to try that again either. I have also voted Liberal and New Democrat. I describe myself as a Red Tory although I'm not exactly sure why. I think I just like the sound of it.

I work somewhere between a third and half my time for the government, although it feels like more. I hope the government appreciates my effort, but if it does, it hasn't bothered to let me know. It would make me feel better if the government dropped me a note that said, "Hey, thanks. This is great. We'll be able to do a lot of wonderful things for the general good with your contribution. You're a heck of a guy. Sincerely, The Government."

This mug's game is to write stuff in the newspaper. Some days I write stuff that is lucid, reasoned, persuasive and that I firmly believe. The next day I look at it and say, "What a crock. This isn't what you believe at all. How could you write such foolishness?"

I lost my virginity to someone I had actually met before. We had gone steady all through acne. Naturally I proposed. Naturally she accepted. It was a bad habit to get into. I started proposing to every girl I went to bed with. All too often, they accepted. I have been married twice and I hope that ends it. I don't want to make a habit of getting married.

I floss my teeth and shower every morning and put on clean underwear when it's available. I can't sleep late any more and wish I could, especially when I have a hangover. I just counted and find I have six books in various stages of being read. It won't surprise me if I don't finish any of them; I am a great beginner of things, but lag in the stretch. The basement is a mess.

I am an Aries, although I can never remember what that's supposed to mean, and will be forty-two in April. My eyes are brown. I watch birds, but haven't done much of it lately and feel the poorer for it. What this mug needs more than anything is a good long walk in the woods. I like opera and country music. The kind of country music I like is the kind you can dance to. I know how to waltz.

I think I waltz pretty well.

Mother cleans up

We had always admired Mother's skills as a housekeeper. She got into corners where the toughest dirt – in any other household – could reasonably have expected to grime out the rest of its days. Once a week – amazing, when I look back on it – she would heave the fridge out from the wall and scrub away at the accumulated cat hairs and grease.

These were the little signs that something out of the ordinary was going on in our house, but you know how it is: you take for granted those closest to you.

Then one evening we were sitting around, Madge and Phil and Father and I, while Mother ironed Father's shirts. Her strokes were sure and smooth. They seemed effortless, so natural that they might have been choreographed in the grand design of the Creation.

When she put down the iron and began to fold the shirt, we found ourselves sitting forward in our seats, our eyes riveted on her every move, or absence of moves. The shirt seemed to assume a life of its own, so deft were her hands. It was flip, flip, flip, pat, and – presto! – the shirt was trim and crisp and folded so finely that a surveyor with a theodolite would have been hard put to find a line that deviated from the true.

We rose spontaneously, adoringly, and applauded until our hands stung. Breathtaking, said Father. A superlative performance, said Madge. Spell-binding, said Phil. A tour de force, said I. Mother blushed and bowed shyly while we screamed for an encore.

Things kind of mushroomed from there. The neighbours were over a couple of nights later and, as if out of the blue, although he had been waiting for exactly the right moment, Father suggested that Mother vacuum the rug.

"Oh, dear," she said, looking a bit embarrassed, but he kept coaxing her and she finally relented, went to the closet, hauled out the Electrolux, set the extension attachment at "shag," plugged it in, turned it on, and set to with a swoosh.

The neighbours eyed one another as if Mother and Father were a few bricks short of a hod, but their scepticism evaporated as they saw the whirring machine in her knowing hands become an instrument as delicate and precise as a surgeon's blade.

Back and forth, back and forth in a mesmerizing rhythm, and although to all eyes the rug had been as clean as a whistle before, it started to assume a pristine quality. It began to look as if it had, just this instant, been delivered from the factory. When she was finished, all the nap, every single individual pile, lay parallel, compass-perfect, as if each had taken a bearing from Polaris.

The neighbours embraced Mother and cried a bit and said things like, "To think we knew you when," and, "We hope you won't forget your friends when you're a star."

It was the first time anyone had said the word out loud, but we were all beginning to suspect we were involved in something bigger than any of us. Father and Madge and Phil and I exchanged glances and felt a little warm behind the eyes.

That Friday, Mother was guest of honour at the Rotary luncheon. She laughed when Father suggested she take along the old wringer washer from the garage and run through a load of socks, but went along with it when he told her that nostalgia was a big turn-on these days.

The Rotary went nuts; they asked endless questions about the strange metal frames – the sock stretchers – to slip the socks over after they'd oozed from the wringer. Then they sang their song to her three times – a local record.

Limited engagements at shopping centres were followed by the grandstand show at the Canadian National Exhibition. That was the first real biggie. That was where she had Madge and Phil pretend to be asleep in twin beds. Mother rushed on stage, shook them awake, then, while they dressed, she packed their lunches, made them both hearty breakfasts, and made both beds with hospital corners and the blankets spread so tautly that when Father – who acted as emcee – dropped a quarter on them, it bounced a good foot in the air. As Madge and Phil hurried offstage, pretending they were off to school, the vast crowd in the grandstand erupted and Mother was engulfed in wild adulation.

From there it was the Merv Griffin Show and that now-legendary moment when Mother spotted a loose button on Merv's cuff and sewed it back on without ever losing the thread – no pun intended – of their conversation about defrosting.

There were invitations for her to dust before the crowned heads of Europe. She wowed North America when she hosted the Academy Awards and shelf-papered the entire stage, polished the silver, and darned a hole in Robert Redford's sweater while passing out the Oscars.

But rifts developed in our happy household. She claimed Father was holding her back when he refused to let her get a cleaning woman. He claimed a cleaning woman was contrary to the philosophy of her act. She said she wanted to start attracting a higher-brow audience and went ahead and got one. Then she said she was going to add a big new finale to the show – she was going to make an omelette without breaking eggs. Father insisted it was impossible. But she did it – how, no one but she will ever know – and that very night she moved out.

She's a big star now. We see her every now and then on TV. We know that, briefly, we were touched by greatness and did not measure up. We miss her, dearly. The house is an awful mess.

Old-fashioned dough

In the lobby of our office building is a large machine – much bigger than a breadbox, about the size of a privy – with an illuminated front and an array of buttons and signal lights. The machine is called an Instant Teller and it is not uncommon to see individuals pressed up against it in digital negotiation for some of the instant money it dispenses.

I don't expect to see the machine around much longer though, because I don't expect this instant money has much of a future. It is true that people in a big way have taken to instant rice and instant coffee and cakes you just whip out of the freezer and hold under your armpit until they are warm enough to serve, but I think with money it is different.

Money has a particular aura about it. People will shun this instant stuff because what they really hanker after is the kind of money Mother used to make.

That was stick-to-your-ribs money, money with real natural goodness all the way through. When a family sat down to a meal made with that old-fashioned money – made from scratch, that was the phrase Mother used – they just about keeled over from it being so nutritious.

Then after supper Mother and Dad and Jack and Susan would sit around and Dad would tell how the money they had just enjoyed was made with an old family recipe that had been passed down from generation to generation and the ingredients were hard work and gumption. "There's nothing sissy about making money," Dad would say, cuffing Jack playfully on the ear.

Mother could make that money go a long way. She could use it to patch Jack's jeans, darn Dad's socks, get shoes re-soled, sew new curtains for Susan's room, and with any leftovers she could make herself a pretty new smock and simmer up a soup that would feed a hardy family for weeks. She used to swear by that money.

"Why, without it we'd starve to death," she used to joke.

And it would last. Every fall Mother would sterilize crates of Mason jars and put down quart after quart of money that she stacked on spiderwebby shelves in the cold room in the basement. She would

167

hum as she did it and the air in the house was warm and sweet with that never-to-be-forgotten smell of prosperity.

Then, when the winter dragged on and there was no fresh money to be found anywhere, she would send Jack or Susan downstairs for a jar of her best preserves. It was lovely to have around. The family always felt it could tough it out because of Mother's resourcefulness.

The local merchants were glad to take it in trade, too. Whenever we needed anything from one of the shops, Mother would just send some money around with Jack or Susan and they could pick up whatever it was. Even the banks seemed happy to get some – but maybe those were just simpler times all around.

Now the banks have gone into the instant money business and, just like any other corporation, they've downgraded the product.

As an experiment, I took one of Mother's old dollars that I happened to have kept in the family Bible, pressed along with my First Communion bow-tie and my first corsage, and went out on the town. With no trouble at all I got in to see a movie – a double feature featuring Randolph Scott, no less – had some popcorn, went out after to the drugstore for a cherry Coke, and still had more than enough for carfare home.

I took the money I had left after carfare and invested it in a cautious company that cares about old-fashioned money called Bell Telephone, and while I waited for that investment to mature, the little bit that was still left I used to buy a bungalow with a patio and a finished rec room.

That's what they mean when they say, "In those days a dollar was a dollar."

The next night I took out one of those new-fangled instant dollars and it said, "You can forget that double-feature-and-a-Coke nonsense, Pops, I wanna go to the disco."

At the disco it wouldn't buy a single thing itself, so I had to keep pulling out more dollars to keep it happy. By the time I'd finished spending that one instant dollar, it had cost me $100.

Once the novelty wears off, people will want the old stuff back.

The Queen, God bless me

About the most tedious cliché of the twentieth century is Andy Warhol's: because of television we'll all be famous for fifteen minutes.

What Warhol didn't consider is that some of us might get our fifteen minutes and blow it. It can happen. I did it.

I don't know why I agreed to go on the *David Frost Show* to talk about the monarchy. I think it might be because aliens from outer space snuck up when I was sleeping and stole my brain. That would certainly help explain why I said what I said on the show.

There were fifteen to twenty of us invited guests (I was paid, I don't know about the others). It wasn't actually a show, but a taping to be broadcast later, or maybe never, which wouldn't surprise me as things turned out.

The format wasn't clear to me as we were settled in the front two rows of seats and perhaps 100 members of the general public filed in and sat behind us. But soon David Frost appeared and we practised clapping on cue. Then we were rolling, at which point it turned out the format was nothing but argle-bargle by whoever wanted to chime in about whether we should have a monarchy or not. A solid hour of it. Good Lord, I thought.

Don't get me wrong. I am not opposed to having a queen, or even a king if it comes to that. I kind of like them. It is just that on the list of things to which I care to give serious thought it comes just after figuring out what a runcible spoon is. That's where I rank it among issues. I don't think of it as pressing.

Not so for much of the rest of the audience, which included a number of ardent would-be republicans and, it seemed, a larger number of vigorous monarchists, most of them pale young men who wore lapel pins and longed for the return of the empire.

I sat in the front row beside a large, volatile woman who gave me the impression that if I got out of line she would sock me in the eye. On my other side sat a distinguished author and civil libertarian whom I won't identify to save her from undue embarrassment caused by the fact that very soon after things got underway she was stricken with a giggling fit she could not control and which came and went, tidally, throughout the taping. On second thought, I will identify her; it was June Callwood.

It was Callwood's behaviour, I maintain, that unhinged me. Maybe it was because halfway through the show she decided to empty her purse and rearrange its contents or maybe because in reply to a question from Frost she barely managed to retain her equilibrium as she said she thought we Canadians like the Queen because she is a frumpy old thing. Or a dumpy old dame. Or something like that. I couldn't take any notes so my quotations aren't exact. I'm trying to give you the gist.

I thought the large woman on the other side was going to sock me in the eye for Callwood being flippant. Anyway, I was not completely in control when Frost turned to me for an opinion and, since I had none, I used a line a friend had given me earlier. "Tell him you don't mind the monarchy, you just think it should be elected."

I thought it was a pretty absurd joke, so I laid it on Frost, who didn't seem to get it and soon had everybody in a hot discussion about the idea of electing a queen and who might be a candidate.

That's when I lost track of things. What with the lights and the stupefying subject and the heated sentiments and Callwood's giddiness, which was rattling the seats, I lost control.

"But seriously, David," I heard myself saying, each word ringing worse than the one before, like a condemned man's footfalls on the gallows steps, "what about those of us who are closet monarchists?"

He looked at me blankly. I wasn't deterred.

"You know, those of us who like to dress up like the Queen?"

Oh dear.

Frost's face sort of filled with turmoil. The audience was stilled, as if one of their number had just committed an unspeakable act. Then, "Oh, bad taste!" shrilled the large woman beside me. "Yucko!" shrieked Callwood, recoiling. Then all was outraged uproar.

No one spoke to me for the rest of the night. And now millions of viewers will think I like to dress up like the Queen. Well, I don't. I've never even tried it.

Smoking

Before lighting a cigarette, I hold the white tissue cylinder in my fingers and squeeze it gently, rolling it back and forth to feel the crinkle of the tobacco inside. Smoking excites all the senses and this first appeal, to the touch, feeling the packed tobacco in its paper sheath, is magnified, carrying as it does the delicious anticipation of all the sensations to come.

I place it between my lips and breathe the first of the cigarette's treasury of smells. Smell is often the best key to the mind's chamber of nostalgia; a whisp of a certain perfume, the aroma of certain foods, of a baseball glove, of the interior of a car, will often flash us back not just to an age when we once felt a special way, but to the day, the hour, sometimes to the very instant, and recreate it in careful detail.

The cigarette's first, unlit smell is brown as the sweetest day of autumn, as ripe as a full haymow with blades of sunlight stabbing through the cracks between the boards, each blade a million galaxies of shimmering motes of dust. And there is a bitterness to it, too, that tweaks the membranes at the back of the nose and freshens them.

Lighting a cigarette would be reward enough, even if there weren't greater rewards in store. The flare of flame. Cupping my hands in a breeze to protect the flame, preserving something so ephemeral long enough to get the cigarette burning, gives me a feeling of triumph – small perhaps, but any triumph is rare – over the elements. Or, in the intimacy of sharing the lighted end of a friend's cigarette and holding it against the tip of my own, I draw deeply until the chemical magic of combustion takes hold.

Seeing the end of my cigarette begin to glow, hearing the near-subliminal hiss as it begins to burn, is a Promethean joy: stealing pleasure from the gods.

There is a paradox in the taste of smoke. It is biting; it is acrid and burning. Freshets of saliva race into the mouth to combat it. The tongue writhes to life, all its taste buds suddenly under sharp attack. The whole mouth is on the alert, wide awake. The loveliness of the taste comes from its contrariness to what the senses instinctively expect. They revel in the surprise, in its pungency. It is as pungent as a cedar fire blazing in a hearth, or the stories hidden away in the best Irish whisky.

Then, Wham! The hit as you inhale. The smoke explodes in the lungs. The smoke detonates in the lungs and you expand into a magnificence you could never otherwise imagine. Oh, Glory. When lightning rips apart the blackness of a storm and leaves a phantom impression of trees bending in the gale and sheeting rain and of the contours of the land that wasn't there before and isn't now – it is that sort of impact you feel.

A faint intoxication invades the brain, takes the rough edges off the knives that pierce it. The echoes of the blast reverberate to the fingertips, to the soles of the feet. The roots of the hair on your scalp vibrate blissfully. Every inch of you, every muscle, gland, joint, organ, every cell in your body is stimulated.

And, following on it like a wave of respite, comes an unfathomable peace that embraces you and holds you sweetly. For a fleeting moment you know how it is to feel complete.

Exhaling creates more shades of expression than any artist ever did with palette and brush. It punctuates, emphasizes, is abrupt, or it is moody, wistful. As winsome as smoke rings. As fanciful as the patterns of clouds browsing across the sky.

When thoughts are vague, shapeless, disinclined to come together, when they dance tantalizingly just beyond the limits of my vision, I exhale and watch the smoke curl sinuously, watch it create shapes in the air. I use it as a map of my imagination; I take my bearings from it. In the delicate smoke ideas crystallize.

After a meal a cigarette heightens the meal, after making love it heightens the love, at the end of a day it heightens the day. Having a cigarette comforts me in my solitude.

I love butting out a cigarette. It has about it a finality; something has been done, done definitely and done well. I love the faint melancholy it brings; that a bit more time has passed and is lost. I love looking forward to my next cigarette.

I love everything there is about smoking. What a shame.

My star is born

In the constellation Hercules, at sky co-ordinates RA 17h 40m 35sd, 37 degrees, 17 minutes, is a star that has been named in honour of me and registered with the International Star Registry.

Its new designation is Homunculus Barbatus, which, roughly translated from the Latin, means short, bearded person. The star is a white dwarf.

One recent clear night, when the stars hung so low you had to brush them aside as you walked, I searched out my star. Looking north I found the Big Dipper and, following the drinking gourd, beyond it the Little Dipper and Polaris, the North Star. Hercules was a few degrees to the right, hunkered down on the far horizon.

The constellation is shaped vaguely like a huntsman down on one knee with his club raised, as if in the act of smashing some small creature to a bloody pulp. In that picture, my star is the belly button.

Up until now, the feature of Hercules that had everybody talking was to be found at roughly the right hip, the globular cluster M13. It contains about half a million stars, the cluster, and is about 100 light years in diameter. The nearest star in it was 34,000 light years from earth the night I looked, but that is changing rapidly since the solar system, of which we are so lordly a part, is rushing toward Hercules at twelve miles per second and eventually will crash into it, screwing up a lot of vacation plans.

As I peered upward at my star, I recalled that Hercules was born of an extramarital affair between Zeus and Alcmene and that after tossing off his twelve labours, he rescued Prometheus who was chained to a rock where an eagle was eating his liver because he had stolen fire from the gods and given it to man, an incident which many big-name scientists dispute but which frosted Zeus's pumpkin nevertheless. And I wondered if my wife would have left me if she had known that some day I would be the owner of a valuable property in outer space.

(If I might throw aside this mask of modesty for a moment, I will admit that I have always wanted to have something named after me, a mountain, a university, a small city, or, if that isn't convenient, a big city, because, let's face it, it's time ordinary guys got some recognition. It's always heads of state or explorers or famous scientists that get things named after them and, if you think about it, they really don't need the exposure because they've already got more money than brains. But an ordinary guy, what's he got? The only achievement in his life is his car needs new radiator hoses. Let's give him a break. Do something nice for him for a change. A star? Well, if that's the best you've got, a star's fine. Now, on with our story.)

Tad and Sylvie had taken shelter from the marauding pygmies in a cave and were huddled together for warmth when the skies parted and a fierce downpour began to pour down. Tad's lips yearningly brushed the back of Sylvie's longing neck and the vein beneath the dirt-stained bandage on his brow began – Wait a minute! Wrong story.

It's time I stopped playing mumblety-peg and came right out and stated where I stand on the question of Creation. Genesis or Big Bang? Well, I don't buy either. What I believe is, I believe there was nothing but darkness in the void, complete darkness, and complete silence was in the void as well.

Then there was a sound of shuffling, as of feet shuffling in bedroom slippers, and then there was a thud. Thud! Like that. Then there was a sound of a voice saying, "Boy, that hurts." Then there was a click, as of a light switch being flicked on and all the stars proceeded to gleam in the firmament. That's the God-stubbing-His-toe-in-the-dark Theory. That's what I believe.

Does my star have planets? Yes, two of them. Are they populated? Yes. One is populated by little tiny grand pianos that make a thrumming sound when they walk; they communicate in Chopin. The other has an atmosphere composed of hogwash and is inhabited by people running for election.

Now here's the deal. That star up there in Hercules' belly button is mine, agreed? So say you step outside for a breath of air and it shines on you? You send me $5 every time that happens, okay? Sounds fair to me.

Freedom, roots, and Waylon Jennings

Bowling along through a big, fat, mysterious, beautiful novel by Mark Helprin called *Winter's Tale*, I came on the words, "Quite possibly there is nothing as fine as a big freight train starting across the country. . . . That's when you learn that the tragedy of plants is that they have roots."

I stopped right there, turned out the light, and lay listening to the wind making its sure-footed way through the night. The wind moving past was murmuring subversive things.

Last week Waylon Jennings was at the CNE for a concert and I went to hear him. He didn't sing my favourite Waylon Jennings' song, "Willie the Wandering Gypsy and Me," maybe because it is too subversive. It goes: "Three fingers of whisky pleasures the drinkers/ And movin' does more than the same thing for me./ Willie he tells me the doers and thinkers/ Say movin' is the closest thing to bein' free."

The birds are packing up, getting ready to go. Swallows are waiting in lines on the hydro wires. The yellowlegs have shown up from the north, lanky sandpipers that wade in the shallows of Corner Marsh and Cranberry Marsh, out beyond Pickering. In his *Keith County Journal*, John Janovy, Jr., a biologist, writes of doing studies along the South Platte River in Nebraska one September when the Creator appeared.

The Creator, wryly enough, had assumed the shape of a red-haired woman and was driving a 1973 baby blue Mustang. "Out on the river bed a lesser yellowlegs lingered and She called to it, 'It's late; get going.' The yellowlegs skittered across the sand before climbing in full-strength flight toward the south." The Creator said to the professor, "You will never really understand My world until you follow the yellowlegs."

The professor didn't quite realize it, but subversion was in the air. He "stood in the knee-deep water and watched the blue Mustang disappear down the highway just as the yellowlegs had disappeared into the sky. 'I have a feeling there is something going on that we're still not even yet quite a part of,'" he said.

In one of the loveliest novels ever written, *Last of the Curlews*, Fred Bodsworth describes the curlew's last moments on its Arctic summering ground:

"There was no reasoning or intelligence involved. The curlew was merely responding in the ages-old pattern of his race to the changing cycle of physiological controls within him. As days shortened, the decreasing sunlight reduced the activity of the bird's pituitary gland. The pituitary secretion was the trigger that kept the reproductive glands pouring sex hormones into the blood stream, and as the production of sex hormones decreased, the bird's aggressive mating urge disappeared and the migratory urge replaced it. It was entirely a physiological process. The curlew didn't know that winter was coming again to the Arctic and that insect eaters must starve if they remained. He knew only that once again an irresistible inner force was pressing him to move."

The city has an itch, a restlessness that keeps it awake nights. Not a symptom it can exactly describe, not something it can exactly scratch. Something, maybe it is something the wind says, speaks to us but we don't know what to make of the message. Perhaps it is not in a language we understand any more. Friends with sons and daughters that have gone off to university this week phone to say nothing much in particular.

Hours later I am still awake. I go to the shelf and take down the most subversive book I own, *Huckleberry Finn*. Huck ends it this way: "But I reckon I got to light out for the Territory ahead of the rest, because Aunt Sally she's going to adopt me and sivilize me and I can't stand it. I been there before."

Dawn coming soon. Soon I must make my rooted way to work. I put on the Waylon Jennings album and listen to him sing about "Willie the Wandering Gypsy and Me." But Waylon – you know, he's not that resolute a subversive. Because on the very next cut he sings,

"Low down freedom, you done cost me / Everything I'll ever lose."

When I heard that I climbed back into bed and finally, I guess, slept.

My father's pyjamas

My father's pyjamas moved in with me. My father came and stayed one night and after he left I found his pyjamas hanging on a hook on the back of the bathroom door. They are white pyjamas with a blue paisley design. They didn't seem in any hurry to leave.

Mine is a one-bedroom apartment in a building inhabited mainly by young people who spend most of their time in Old Vienna beer commercials. I would have thought my father's pyjamas would find their ways frivolous and noisy. Some of these young people are not great respecters of their parents' pyjamas. "They don't even wear pyjamas of their own," I told my father's pyjamas.

But they just hung there, unfazed by the suggestion that they were out of their element. I put them in the laundry. I thought of the philosophical irony: the child is father to the father's pyjamas. I took them out of the dryer, folded them, and put them in a drawer. And then I started to feel just awful.

"Comes a time in a life – " I debated with myself. "Comes a time in a life when pyjamas aren't much use to anybody any more. That's when, as it may be, they just get washed and folded and put away in a drawer.

"Oh, sometimes they get a bit of extra use as a duster or as a rag to polish shoes. But I couldn't let that happen to my father's pyjamas. The family wardrobe always had its pride. Even at its most thread-bare, it was too proud to go into a rummage sale. It could always fend for itself. At the very least I have some responsibility for caring for my father's pyjamas.

"After all, flannelette is thicker than water."

I took them out of the drawer and put them on the couch beside me and we watched the news. I had to switch from the CBC news to Global, though, because my father's pyjamas are accustomed to watching Global. "That's all right," I said. "News is news."

When it was over, I spread my father's pyjamas out on the couch and went into the bedroom and climbed into bed.

I lay awake for ages. Sleep wouldn't come. All I could think of was my father's pyjamas on that narrow, lumpy couch. Finally I got up, took the pyjamas off the couch, put them in my bed, and tucked them in. "It's all right," I said. "You need a rest. A little discomfort doesn't bother me at all." I went and lay down on the couch.

Until my father's pyjamas came I hadn't realized how small the apartment was. Now it seemed that everywhere I turned they were there. Spread over a chair with the paper on their lap. Draped over the shower rail when I was in a rush to shower and get to the office. Listening to the radio when I wanted to play a record. Knotting and unknotting their ties disapprovingly while I explained why I was late getting home.

When in need of warm companionship it was my habit to drop by an Old Vienna beer commercial, sweet-talk a waif, and invite her back to my apartment for a little hanky-panky.

"What's that?" the waif hissed as we came in one night.

My father's pyjamas were seated at the table, a game of solitaire spread out before them. "Just my father's pyjamas," I explained. "Pay no attention to them."

In any case, I took them and hung them in the bathroom. It did no good. My whining entreaties were as much use as a candle trying to boil an iceberg. "I'm sorry," she said. "I just don't feel right, knowing your father's pyjamas are in there."

I sent her back to the beer commercial in a cab and brought my father's pyjamas out and settled them beside me. Together we watched Global news. "It's all right," I said. "Having my father's pyjamas is company enough. What need have I of transient, insincere relationships with women?"

But despite my best intentions, my father's pyjamas started to get on my nerves. I would raise my voice when I spoke to them. Sometimes when I went off to work I left them in a heap. Soon I wasn't coming home for meals. I stayed in bars until all hours and rolled home full of abuse for the lint they left everywhere.

One day I came home to find the Goodwill truck in front of the building and the Goodwill man coming out of my apartment with my father's pyjamas over his arm. "Ingrate," sneered the Goodwill man. My father's pyjamas didn't look back as they left.

Appliance psychology

A new appliance, a vacuum cleaner, has come to live with us and we are very happy. All except the electric broom. The electric broom is in a sulk and refuses to come out of the electric broom closet.

But if the electric broom hadn't gone and got completely choked full of huge hairy dustballs and something gummy and disgusting, the new vacuum cleaner wouldn't have come to live with us, so it has only itself to blame.

The vacuum cleaner is the first new appliance to move in since the hair dryer. The hair dryer had "Professional Model" written on its side and behaved quite arrogantly toward the other appliances. Then one night it went berserk and tried to burn my head to a cinder.

It obviously thought itself suited to higher things than my humble locks. It spat sparks and howled and behaved very badly and while I firmly believe that appliances respond best to love, they must also know their place, so I stomped it to bits on the bathroom floor.

The new vacuum cleaner is cute as a button. It is not much bigger than the toaster; in fact I noticed that the toaster blushed and got quite short of breath when I introduced them. I better keep an eye on those two. You never know what might pop up! Dear me. Anyway, I'll give them a good talking to if things start to get cosy.

My friends think I'm a big silly because I talk to my appliances but – and I'll bet if they did some experiments on this down at the university they'd find out I'm right – appliances do a better job, use less electricity, and require fewer repairs if you talk to them in a soft, affectionate, and encouraging voice. Tell them how glad you are to see them, tell them how spiffy they look. Before long they act as if a horsepower or two had been added to their little motors.

I don't speak to the stove and fridge, at least not unless spoken to. They were here when I moved in and are major appliances so I respect their privacy. But the others, my own dear little appliances, we chitter and chatter and burble all day long and sometimes we share jokes and laugh so hard we blow fuses.

Look at them gathered around me now, the burger-popper, the orange juicer, the espresso maker, the toaster, and the shiny new vacuum cleaner. Everything is getting along beautifully and nothing is saying anything unkind about the burger-popper. Thank goodness.

The burger-popper was given to us some time ago and has never fit in very well. To tell the truth, it's never been used. You see, there's something – well, I don't want to sound prejudiced, but there's something that strikes me as a little bit odd about an appliance that is designed to pop corn and cook hamburgers. It seems a little – I don't know – bipolar.

Doesn't it seem so to you? What if the toaster also beat eggs or the orange juicer also pressed my trousers? I know it is asking perhaps a bit too much for an appliance in today's household to be exactly one thing or another, but that's the way I was brought up. My mother's iron ironed and her mother's deep-fryer fried deeply, and that was that. Things were straightforward.

But even the espresso maker, which is quite Continental and should be sophisticated about these things, turns up its steam jet, the one that is used to whoosh milk to a heavenly froth for capuccino, and refuses to acknowledge the burger-popper when they are out on the counter together.

Lord knows, I try. I really do. But when I get a burger patty all carefully seasoned and patted out and go to put it on the burger-popper I am suddenly swept by doubt and wonder whether I wouldn't rather have a heaping bowl of popcorn instead. And vice-versa. It's an appliance, and I love it, but there's something about it that turns me into a seething bundle of indecision.

But we had a lovely time. I switched on the new little vacuum cleaner and it roared like a brave and tidy lion. The other appliances hummed appreciatively and in no time at all the place was gleaming.

Later, when everything was at last unplugged and the apartment was dark, I took the electric broom out of the electric broom closet and threw it off the balcony. We don't need its sort around.

Homely marvels

I said to Ma – Ma was doing the ironing at the time – I said, "Ma, nobody ever gave nobody the Nobel prize for ironing."

Ma didn't say nothing. She was watching *As The World Turns* and you could light her on fire while she was watching *As The World Turns* and it wouldn't distract her.

Once or twice while I've watched her, she's been watching *As The World Turns* and not watching where she was ironing and she's ironed her hand. Her left hand – Ma's right-handed. She never even took her eyes off the screen. Just kept right on ironing.

They keep handing out the Nobel prize for medicine and for peace and the like and so far as I can see there's still all sorts of sick people and wars, etc., in the world, but there's not many people going around with their clothes all wrinkled, which seems to me to mean that ironing is a force to be reckoned with that hasn't been. "Where's the tributes for ironers?" I asked Ma.

"Or for haberdashery?" I went on. A person could invent a cure for the quinzy tomorrow and the Nobel prize bigwigs would have a van around by noon and workmen would be carting his prize up the front steps and piling it on the porch. "But where's there a statue of the guy that invented socks? Tell me that?"

You ever stop to think about socks? Note, for instance, how many of them you've got when you've got a pair of them. Two. Now count your feet and, except in the rare instances where you might be equipped with only one or maybe three, the statistical average is two. Two feet, two socks. Talk about planning bang-on.

If anybody ever planned that well in government, half the bureaucrats would be pounding the pavement looking for jobs, of which there aren't any, which is why I am glad to have philosophy as a sideline since it can be performed right here on the couch in the afternoon.

The thing I have to admire about socks even more than what I believe is called pairity is the fact that they are closed at one end and open at the other. Coming up with that took what goes down as genius in my book. Why, otherwise you'd pull one on and, zip, it'd be up around your waist and no good at all versus the wintry blast at foot level. Or it'd ride up like your nightgown, which is not what I would say was a garment that was designed with a great deal of common sense from that point of view.

"Or, while we're on the subject, housewares," I said to Ma. I had noticed when she was doing the vacuuming before *As The World Turns* came on and she had to turn off the Electrolux that the invention of the vacuum cleaner bag had sure taken a lot of the toil and worry out of tidying up the joint.

"Must have been quite a sight in the old days, eh?" I said, but she just kept whaling away at Pa's big overalls, which he always liked to wear with razor-sharp creases so his friends in the Unemployment Insurance line wouldn't think he was some kind of ne'er-do-well. I might as well've been talking to a ballpeen hammer.

Imagine it. The vacuum cleaner sucking away to beat the band, inhaling everything that wasn't nailed down, and if there wasn't a bag there to gather in all the stuff and hold on to it, the vacuum would just shoot it right on through and spew the corruption all over creation.

They can dish up all the Nobel prizes for electron fritzing and nuclear futzing they want, but it won't mean nothing to me as much as if they'd passed out the laurel to the unsung whoever that single-handed has kept this living room from turning into a complete pigsty.

"Oven mitts! Hey, Ma! Some time you tell me about oven mitts!" You could never hoist dinner out of the oven if it wasn't for oven mitts or their forebearers, pot-holders. Burn your hands to a cinder if it wasn't for them. Every time you want to grab the roast or the scalloped potatoes, aiyee! Total agony.

Way I look at it, whoever invented oven mitts has kept the world from starving to death from having to wait until the stuff had gone stone cold and the Nobel prize is scarcely credit enough for that.

"Speaking of which, Ma," I said, "a person could starve right now for all anybody cares." If she heard me, she never let on.

Cruising in Serena Gundy Park

If you watch the trees very closely these days, not the evergreens, but the willows, the maples, the oaks, you can see their outlines blur against the sky and sometimes you blink because you think your eyes have slipped out of focus. The prickly outlines blur as the buds get leafy inclinations and start to yawn and stretch. Even trees look a little bleary when they first wake up.

If you put your ear to the ground, you can hear the earth working. It is a waking sound, too. It only slowly insinuates itself into your awareness, the way a difference in breathing rhythms does as someone beside you surfaces from a long sleep.

Those are kind of languid images. Maybe we need something a little stronger. This wasn't a winter to wake from so much as a winter to survive. Instead of stretching and scratching, we should be counting our limbs to see if they're all still there.

If you look at the hillsides that face north and compare them with the hillsides that face south, the north-facing slopes are still in the snow-sogged, chill shadows of winter. The south-facing slopes are brown, leaf-littered, waiting for spring to stop spinning its wheels. If you walk up the middle of the valleys, you can walk one foot in winter, one foot in spring – it is sort of a de-seasonalized zone: hostilities have ceased but we have yet to hear the terms of the armistice.

These are notes from a vagrant morning in Serena Gundy Park.

If there is a prettier name for a park anywhere, I have yet to hear it. And if you know what's good for you, you will go out there and bob up and down on the swooping suspension footbridge that carries you into the park across the Don River. If you are still in a foul humour after bobbing up and down, then throw yourself off the bridge and dash your brains out on the rocks below; you are beyond help, anyway.

Romance is in the air. A woodpecker drums a come-hither drum on a hollow tree over there somewhere. Cardinals make piercingly libidinous suggestions to any bit of fluff that blows by on the southwest breeze. Robins flap and squawk and scoot from under hedges and low cedars like teen-agers caught making out in the driveway. Every crow that beats across the sky is carrying a bunch of thatch to thatch a shack to shack up in.

At the end of a woody cove, a shallow ravine – more like a gully – pitches down through the trees. It is filled with snow and well marked with tracks of toboggans, children's sleighs, the wobbly downhill courses and herringbone uphills of cross-country skiers. But the tracks, while clear, are no longer sharp. They are softened, the way memories – at least pleasurable memories – are softened as we get farther from the original experience. And they last much longer than the unpleasurable memories that melt rapidly out of mind around them.

Spring is a lot farther along with its cleaning than some people I could name. This year I had planned to go through the backs of closets and cupboards – not as a piker, either. I planned to go through those cupboards under the sinks in the kitchen and the bathroom, the places where things accumulate that require cleaning agents not stocked in mere supermarkets.

Those are the places where you find the worst buildups of envy. Unless you get rid of envy almost as soon as it appears, you may find yourself stuck with it for life. Jealousy is annoying; it leaves sticky stains on everything it touches, but although it is unsightly, it is not nearly as bad as envy. Generally it can be removed with soapy water and a stiff brush.

I couldn't find envy anywhere that spring has cleaned; everything appeared quite content with whatever it was. That is my plan when I have my cleaning finished: to be quite content with whatever it is I happen to be. All I hope is that under this grimy envy I find I'm as rich as Conrad Black.

I sashayed past a herd of picnic tables grazing on soggy patches of grass and up a winding walk to a low, stone gate with a plaque on it inscribed, "This was Serena Gundy's garden. She loved it and would be happy to share it with others."

Imagination, green and singing, thrives there.

10
Life's Not Like That

Take heart

To: All line managers and sales personnel
From: President and Chief Executive Officer, Asphodel Fibreheart Systems, Inc.
Re: Marketing Strategy

The new model lines of Asphodel Fibreheart will be going into production soon and it is time we reviewed developments to date and considered how best to position ourselves in the highly competitive artificial heart field. The ad agency is testing two approaches we hope will make Asphodel in hearts what Aspirin is in pain-relievers: *the* name. One is, "You gotta have heart, so make it Asphodel," and the other is, "Asphodel – and the beat goes on."

Efforts to establish an artificial heart fund to assist Research & Development have met with limited success since governments and major funding institutions have only been willing to contribute artificial dollars. Until this can be remedied, plans to equip a senior citizens' club with Turbo-charged Fibrehearts prior to the first assault on Mount Everest by old-age pensioners have been put on the back burner. We will keep you advised.

In the meantime R&D is concentrating its efforts on a digital read-out that will provide up-to-the-minute information on all vital signs, plus time, weather, and traffic reports. Consideration is being given to replacing the current system of warning lights with a computerized conscience that says, "Uh, oh. Easy there," and "Slow down, pal," and "You have just red-lined on cholesterol," in both French and

English. A special adapter will be available to start the coffeemaker in the morning.

In order to counter outrageous claims of vitality made by our competitors and to allay fears of potential customers that Asphodel Fibreheart can't go the distance, long-term research is being channelled into two interrelated streams. We are confident that by year-end Asphodel will be able to offer an optional package guaranteeing everlasting life. This will be a major breakthrough and will open up broad new markets since, while our heart will last forever, other body parts will deteriorate markedly after a millenium or two and need replacement. The demand for artificial hands, feet, digestive tracts, memories, etc. will increase enormously, underscoring our contention that the world of prosthetic devices is in its infancy.

In that regard, we foresee generations of people composed entirely of Asphodel products, running smoothly and efficiently and seeking repair and maintenance at an international chain of Asphodel service centres. The idea of artificial children produced by artificial insemination in artificial wombs is not far-fetched. "Asphodel – the family that works" is an intriguing approach.

But since our polls and data analysis show a significant proportion of the population wearies of life after a few thousand years and since a number of religious organizations have expressed reservations, we expect to offer an alternative option: The Asphodel Afterlife. In keeping with tradition, this afterlife will come in two product lines, one involving wings and harps and peace beyond imagining, while the other will be endless torment, depending on customer preference. Afterlife will be organized along the lines of the Club Mediterrannee and offer group rates.

Our New Products Division is exploring the as-yet theoretical realm of artificial emotions. "Happiness" could be a market-beating program in trying economic times, as could "Optimism." Asphodel will not only garner valuable publicity but will put an end to world hunger if plans to produce an artificial feeling of having eaten far too much come to fruition. Then there is Project X. While it is top secret, let me just say that an integrated-circuit micro-soul would leave our competitors down the track.

Finally, we are making every effort to deal with the recurring problem of customers with artificial hearts who keep falling deeply in love with manufactured goods. We have been somewhat embarrassed by reports that some Asphodel users become intensely aroused whenever their washing machines begin the spin cycle. And the story about the man in Saskatchewan and the combine harvester was a case of media overreaction. Refer press inquiries to head office.

Beware of the dog

Whenever I'm in the supermarket checkout line I take a moment to scan the headlines on *The National Examiner*, an influential tabloid, to see if anybody has made contact with Elvis Presley or done anything else of similar newsworthiness that you can be sure the rest of the media will hush up. When somebody gets in touch with Elvis it will be a front-page story in *The National Examiner*.

And it won't necessarily be some raving lunatic who regularly hears voices on the boogabooga network. It might easily be a cabinet minister or a prominent industrialist placing a call who by mistake hits the button on the touch-tone phone that has an asterisk on it and a phone rings at the other end and Elvis picks it up and says, "Hello?"

That button shouldn't be allowed. Okay, so it might put you in touch with Elvis, but it might as easily honk the klaxon at Strategic Air Command HQ in Omaha, Nebraska, and scramble the bombers and start The Big One. Having nuclear first-strike capability hanging on the kitchen wall makes me uneasy.

So far, we've been lucky. And nobody of any consequence has talked to Elvis, or at any rate *The National Examiner* hasn't run the story yet. But I did see a headline the other day that caught my attention. It said, "Is Your Pet An Alien From Outer Space?" It's the kind of question that, once it gets asked, starts to eat at you.

"Listen," I whispered to my wife when I got home, "have you given serious consideration to the possibility that the dog is an alien from outer space?"

"Why are you whispering?" she said.

"Shhhh, keep your voice down," I said. "We don't want the dog to hear." I told her it was important that we go on living normally. Just go about our daily routine of eating, sleeping, and going to work, always taking pains not to let on to the dog that we suspect it of being an extraterrestrial. "But we'll keep an eye on it, okay? Surreptitiously, we'll study its behaviour."

"The behaviour you should study if you want that dog to live to see summer," my wife said, "is its behaviour in digging up the backyard and eating the daffodil bulbs. It has already eaten all the daffodil bulbs and is starting on the tulip bulbs. There are holes out there you could lose a streetcar in."

"Don't be silly," I told her. "Streetcars don't come anywhere near our backyard. But wait! Those holes might be something. Remember in *2001*, that great big black thing, that plinth or whatever it was? How it floated through space and appeared mysteriously and was some form of intergalactic communication?"

"There's nothing mysterious about the appearance of those holes," she said. "Your dog is stripmining the backyard. That's all. Didn't there used to be a garage out there?"

"And remember *The Chariots of The Gods*?" I said. "Those gigantic prehistoric landing strips and other unexplained earthworks in South America? That's scientific fact, for God's sake. They really exist! That's what the dog is doing. Those holes are signals. He's flashing signals to the rest of the aliens up there."

But she had left the room. I made some notes: Eats sticks. Despite full ration of kibble. Maybe earth-dog diet inadequate. Maybe needs cellulose. Explains why eats cellophane off cigarette packages. Cellulose in socks? Check first thing in morning. Also, if aliens have superior intelligence why dog not learned to ask to go out when has to relieve self? If alien, why has to relieve self? Call Carl Sagan first thing in morning.

I shook my wife awake at 4 a.m. "Do you hear typing?" I whispered.

"No. Leave me alone," she said.

"Have you noticed if the dog hangs around the typewriter? Where is the dog anyway?"

"Under the bed where it always sleeps. Shut up," she said.

"Do you notice a sort of a strange glow coming from under the bed?" I asked. "Sort of greenish?"

No answer. I'm beginning to wonder about my wife. She appears to stonewall a lot of my inquiries. Maybe she and the dog are in cahoots. I am going to pass that on to *The National Examiner*. "Toronto Man Wed To Alien From Outer Space." That should sell some papers.

A primer on bed-making

I talked to a man the other day who had suddenly become a bachelor. He found it trying. Women take such things in their stride. When women suddenly become spinsters there are support systems ready and waiting. But a man who suddenly becomes a bachelor finds himself on his own.

The man was eager to end his bachelor status because it was more than he could handle. "I don't even know how to make the bed. I'm afraid I'll get it apart and never get it back together again," he said. For want of a nail, I thought, Rome was you know what.

It is all right to rush into marriage again for the right reasons. Meeting a woman with a considerable fortune is as right a reason as there is. But not because there is a ring around the tub or the dishes are dirty or the bed shows no inclination to make itself.

Having suddenly become a bachelor myself on several occasions and having become so good at it that if it was an Olympic event I'd be in the medals, I am going to pass on some of the life skills I have attained so that my fellow man might be better able to cope.

Life Skill No. 1: Making the Bed

1. First, identify the bed. One of the piles of stuff in your place of residence is likely the bed. Other piles might be incoming laundry, outgoing laundry, winter clothes not yet put away, and miscellaneous. Try to remember which pile you were in when you woke up this morning. Odds favour that being a good place to start, even though it is now evening.

Burrow into a pile. If you discover a mattress and/or a headboard, then you're well on your way. (Tip: the bedroom is the best place to look, unless it is you who has left the matrimonial home and set up housekeeping on your own, in which case the bed could be anywhere. Maybe you don't have a bed. Maybe you slept on the couch. Were you even home last night? Well? Were you?)

2. Put up a sign with an arrow pointing to the bed, if you find it. You can tack it to the wall or suspend it by string from the ceiling. This will save valuable time should you ever decide to make the bed again. Also it will allay self-doubt. Ninety per cent of bed-making is confidence. If you doubt you can do it, you face a self-imposed obstacle. If you doubt that you can locate the bed in the midst of such a mess, you probably can't. If you don't even know whether you were home last night, then you're licked.

3. Separate into components. These are, usually, bedspread, blankets, sheets, and pillows. Any other objects found in the bed, e.g., a pitching wedge, a half-eaten box of Dad's cookies, will be dealt with in Step 4. Bed components can be marked for ease of identification but in time you will recognize them.

4. Don't take foreign objects found in bed and put them on the floor. Say one evening you find a pitching wedge in the bed (see Step 3) and say you put it on the floor. Say another time you find a half-eaten box of Dad's cookies and put it with the pitching wedge. And the next time it's all your Waylon Jennings records. And then it's the TV remote control. And then a wet towel from when you had a shower before going to work. And you put them all together on the floor. Do you know what you've done? You've created another pile. That's irresponsible. Take everything into the kitchen and put it on the counter where you can sort it tomorrow. Don't put it on top of the dishes, otherwise you'll never find them and have to eat the pizza right out of the box.

5. Seeing as you're in the kitchen, rinse out a glass and pour yourself a drink. When we are tense, anxiety compounds itself. Tense ballplayers can't hit the ball; tense surgeons cut off more than they had bargained for. A tense bed-maker is liable to get tangled in the components and bring who knows what harm to himself. When you are a bachelor nobody cares if you have a drink to relax before you make the bed. Or if you have two.

6. Might as well sit down while you finish it. Might as well see what's on television. The news? Is it that late already? You could've sworn it – thworn ith – thornth – thzzzzzz. When you live alone nobody cares if you snore.

7. It is dawn. You have wakened in an armchair. Maybe that's where you slept the night before. Have you got a clean shirt for work?

Getting the bird

There was a news report the other day about police breaking down the door of an east-end apartment to reach a little girl they could hear screaming in anguish and distress. When the officers got to her they discovered she was in an agony of fear because her budgie had been injured. The budgie had been injured when the little girl stepped on its head.

When I read that I sat bolt upright on the divan.

I know a thing or two about budgies. I used to keep budgies. Once I even built a special breeding cage for the budgies I had and imagined myself growing wealthy as a budgie breeder. Not that they ever did any breeding. They just billed and cooed and left it at that.

But I studied them carefully nevertheless and you couldn't have told me much about budgies that would surprise me. Unless you told me you had injured your budgie by stepping on its head.

If you have never kept budgies you might think stepping on a budgie's head was a common occurrence. It isn't. In all the time I kept budgies I never stepped on one of their heads. You might think, Oh, probably you did once, probably one time when you got up in the night to go to the bathroom or get a glass of milk and didn't look where you were going you stepped on a budgie's head and then forgot about it by morning.

But it's not the sort of thing you would easily forget. In the morning there would be a senseless budgie with a footprint on its head. The sight would jog your memory. You could claim you didn't know how it got there, the footprint, but it would be a lie.

Never did I step on a budgie's head unintentionally. I never even did it intentionally, though God knows I tried often enough.

You get a couple of budgies refusing to go along with your scheme to become fabulously wealthy as a budgie breeder and you can become awfully annoyed. You watch hour upon hour of billing and cooing when your dreams rest on egg production and you can be moved to consider drastic measures. You change enough newspapers in the bottom of a budgie's cage and end up with nothing to show for it but more newspapers to change and even if you are the most reasonable person on earth there comes a day when something snaps and you can't help yourself. You want to step on the budgie's head.

It happened to me. But until I read about it in the paper, I would have sworn it couldn't be done.

It always seemed to me to be in a budgie's nature to avoid having its head stepped on. An instinct. A budgie usually perches in places where it is impossible to get at, the drapery track or the rim of a lampshade. Or it might perch on your finger, in which case you will end up rolling around on the floor comforting a stepped-on finger and weeping bitter tears while the budgie, a picture of unconcern, looks on from the top of the bookshelves.

Or it might perch on your shoulder and nibble your earlobe, in which case it is no problem at all to wind up and take a sock at it, but when you are in the state you are in by the time you are driven to step on a budgie's head, there is little real satisfaction in punching one.

Compounding the difficulty is that budgie keepers frequently, in their hysteria, misjudge their bird. They imagine it is as dopey as it looks. This can be a fatal mistake. Coroners' files are stuffed with cases where people crashed through windows while trying to step on the head of a budgie that was perched on the sill or plunged down elevator shafts or were sliced in two by freight trains.

A person whose senses have been worn bald by a budgie can easily come to believe the budgie is a malevolent force, attempting to lure him to his destruction, perhaps out of revenge for making it live in a cage or for badgering it to say, "Pretty birdie, pretty birdie." There is no wicked intent a person that far gone in budgie dementia won't attribute to his pet. Budgies are vicious and not to be trusted.

I congratulate the little girl, just nine years old, for her amazing and courageous effort. And I know why she was wailing so piteously. She tried and failed. Now she knows the budgie will get her.

Inflation

"That's it. They're not going to get another red dime out of me," she said.

"Red dime?" he said.

"I've had it with those outfits," she said.

"It used to be a red cent. I guess this is one of the ravages of inflation. It is no longer worth those outfits' time to be out for every red cent they can get. Now they want every red dime. If it keeps up we'll be down to our last thin dollar," he said.

"All we talk about any more is money. How it evaporates if you leave it out in the air. Yet I worry about it all the time. Do you still love me even though I am so foolish?" she said.

"Of course I love you. Inflation might eat into our financial security, but it will never erode my love for you. I love you a bushel and a peck," he said.

"Is that a pre-inflationary bushel and a peck, or is it measured at current rates? At current rates, that would mean you loved me only about a tablespoonful when we set out together on the inflationary spiral. Yet you swore then that you loved me a bushel and a peck.

Were you lying to me? Were you leading me on? Or did you, in fact, love me a bushel and a peck and has your love for me failed to keep pace?" she said.

"My love has kept pace. My pre-inflationary love for you was a bushel and a peck and I only mentioned it now because I am a sentimental slob. In fact, because of the ravages of inflation it has increased to about four metric tonnes and has to be hauled around in a tractor-trailer. I never knew such love was possible," he said.

"How tragic that you should care for me so. It is too much. Too much love is constricting. Once there was a time when I would have thought a truckful of love was the most romantic thing I could imagine. But now it smothers me. It makes me feel trapped. I need to be free to be my own person. With you loving me that much I won't be able to realize my self-potential," she said.

"It is all very confusing," he said.

"It is confusing because despite the separateness that I need in our union, we must still cling to each other, knowing it is the only way we can keep the wolf from the door," she said.

"I'm afraid those were the Good Old Days when the wolf was at the door. A ravenous, vicious wolf with burning eyes that howled at the moon and nipped at our heels and threatened to devour us if we stumbled so much as once – why, that was as comforting as a pussycat asleep on the hearth, compared to now. Inflation has maddened a whole pack of wolves and they have us surrounded. There's nowhere we can run. And besides wolves there are crocodiles and man-eating tigers and bear markets and vipers and adders and God knows what. I'd give anything for a mere wolf at the door," he said.

"There, there. We having nothing to fear but fear itself," she said.

"Well, take a good look at that fear. Once it just went bump in the night. Now it is in wide-screen 70-mm with Dolby Sound. It might be all we have to fear, but it is more than enough," he said.

"We truly are happy. We have songs in our hearts and smiles on our lips. We have our pleasures. A good book. The television. We have good friends and glad thoughts and a dash of gin when the spirit craves it. We have the full rich inner lives of true happiness," she said.

"Ah, yes. I remember you saying those very words when we first set out," he said.

"I did? Oh, dear. Now you mention it, I did. And it hasn't changed one bit, has it? Same old songs, same old smiles, same old pleasures.

Same old friends, same old thoughts. Same old inner lives. And the gin doesn't work nearly as well. This might have been happiness once, but now it is sorrow. Happiness wasn't indexed. Now that I think about it, what I am is desolate. With a life this bleak, who wouldn't be depressed?" she said.

"Forget all the inflationary talk. Enjoy this lovely summer's day," he said.

"I would, except it is no lovelier or summery than lovely summer's days used to be. The weather hasn't improved at all," she said.

"You're right. And I'm afraid we're in for more of the same," he said.

Next stop kingdom come

It was shortly after the lunch hour and the people assembling on the subway platform wore the freeze-dried faces we put on in the company of strangers with whom we intend to share as little as possible on a fleeting journey to each of our separate, private destinations.

Sounds were muffled, subterranean. A westbound train rushed in, the trainman whistled, it rushed away. It left behind a shuffling whisper that diminished as the passengers who got off made their way upward toward Yonge Street. Newcomers trickled on to the eastbound platform and soon it was crowded. The train was taking its time.

A tall man in a TTC uniform, a maroon coat with a shoulder flash that said "Inspector," arrived and stood near me. His bearing was erect, stiff, that of a man who takes inspecting seriously. His hands were clasped behind his back.

The wait went on. There were vague grumbles, verging on impatience. People threaded past cautiously, looking for room to stand.

Then things happened. There was a rising gust of air that meant the train was finally coming. There was an indistinct noise. A thump. A thunk. As if something big had been dropped and landed heavily. There were voices shouting. "Oh, God!" "Oh, God!" "She's fallen!" "For God's sake, cut the power." And the train boomed into the light at the far end of the station.

Fifteen feet from me a stricken face, a woman's, rose over the edge of the platform from the track bed four feet below. Her lips were peeled back, her jaws gaped. Her hands reached out, clawing uselessly across the tiles, trying to pull herself up. There was a metallic shriek that might have been the train's brakes. Figures converged. They crouched at the edge of the platform. One was the maroon-clad inspector.

"Get her!" "Get her!" The figures grabbed, heaved. Jerked up like a wriggling fish, she was still in the air when the decelerating train streaked by, inches from her heels.

My stomach heaved. I fought down an urge to retch. My hand was over my mouth. Other people clutched their hearts, held their hands over their mouths. The inspector held the woman by the shoulders and was talking quietly, close to her face, the way a trainer talks to a dazed fighter who has just been battered in a round. She looked as if she had no idea what had happened.

Very few did. Beyond our crowded little semicircle no one else on the platform had seen anything. Over the noise of the approaching train they had heard nothing. The people on the train had arrived from some other context entirely. The total lack of concern on the faces that had whizzed in and come to rest on the very spot where something terrible had almost happened was somehow startling.

The trainman whistled. We shuffled aboard.

So did the woman who had fallen on the tracks. Whatever her schedule had been before she stumbled and fell, nothing had changed. The train that nearly drove her to kingdom come now carried her east toward the Danforth.

A friend of mine is turning fifty. The other day a young woman asked her how she felt about it. My friend said not so hot. She didn't especially care for what age was doing to her body, to her energy, to her enthusiasm, to her perspective. She didn't like the feeling that most of the experiences life had to offer her had already been offered. She didn't like the idea that it was going to end and she was probably closer to the end than to the beginning.

The person who had asked the question was shocked; she clutched her heart, held her hand over her mouth. "Don't say that," she told my friend.

My friend was put out by this. "If she didn't want to know, why did she ask?"

For some reason these two images become linked together in my mind. A terrible end roaring down and someone snatching us to safety at the last possible instant. A natural end creeping up and nobody on the platform to pull us out of the way.

I come back to the lines quoted in *Harper's* magazine by a writer contemplating the imminence of nuclear doom. They were spoken by Albert the Alligator in the old Pogo comic strip. "A man can't live his whole life in fear of ten seconds of boom and whango."

Everything goes

Notes of a clerk at a garage sale:

Proprietors of garage sales find themselves in a dilemma. Are they trying to make a lot of money or are they trying to get rid of a whole lot of junk? Inventory clearance vs. maximization of profits. You have four yellow, globular Happy Face coffee mugs. They are bric-a-brac atrocities and haven't been out of the cupboard since they arrived as gifts. They sit on a trestle table on the front porch marked fifty cents each. A buyer offers $1 for the four. What do you do? Hold out and maybe end up stuck with the mugs or sell them at half price? (Resolution in this instance: took the money and ran. Would have done the same if the buyer had offered ten cents a cup. A nickel.)

It is amazing the kind of junk people will buy. A paperweight shaped like the CN Tower for twenty-five cents. Fifteen identical instant coffee jars with orange tops, ten cents each. An implement shaped like a medieval battle axe that is either an ice-pick or a cheese knife or a letter opener, for $1. Or – the other side of the garage-sale coin – it's amazing the kind of junk people accumulate. A paperweight shaped like the CN Tower. Fifteen identical instant coffee jars with orange tops. An implement shaped like a medieval battle axe that is either an ice-pick or a cheese knife or a letter opener.

A yellow police cruiser pulled up first thing Saturday morning and a constable, gun slung on one hip, nightstick on the other, came up the walk adjusting his cap. Uh-oh. Did we need a permit to run a garage sale? Were we going to get busted? He bought two green lawn chairs. He put them in the trunk of the cruiser and drove off. He was our first customer.

Commotion at the sale on the neighbouring porch. Much shifting and rearranging. A man has bought the table the sale goods were displayed on. A time later there was a commotion on our porch. A woman has bought a cat that had been resident in the house for years. In business they say everything is for sale if you come up with the right price. What next?

When people are buying hand over teakettle I have an urge to rush out and buy a whole bunch more stuff to sell. Then I'd probably sell it at half what it cost. It is a sale, after all. This is what is referred to in retailing as a breathtaking lack of business acumen. It is why it never once occurred to my father that I might take over his drugstore. When you get down to it, it is the difference between me and any Eaton you'd care to shake a stick at.

Garage sales bring out the impulsive in people. A young man relaxes luxuriously in a saggy green armchair that is sadly in need of upholstering. The chair is marked $25. "This chair is fabulous, but all I've got is $15," he says, holding up three fives. Sold. As I help him carry it to his station wagon he says, "I wonder what my wife will say when she sees it?"

Some customers specialize and don't waste any time. They pull up to the curb, wind down a window, and holler, "Got any china?" "Got any jewelry?" Some people tell you this is the fourth or fifth or eighth sale they have been to today. They have the ads clipped from *The Star* and are making a circuit. Some people make garage sales an outing, a hobby. Before long you can spot the pros, used furniture dealers and the like. Most have vans; some leave the engines of the vans running. They can whiz through half a lifetime's accumulation of whatnots and be gone in under a minute.

Is there haggling? There is lots of haggling. Also psychology. A "Souvenir of Expo 67" tray is marked $1. A man offers fifty cents. I tell him he's breaking my heart. I tell him my father brought the tray with him from the old country. We settle for seventy-five cents.

The last customer chances to be a guy I haven't seen in ages. We used to tear around together ten years and more ago. Once we got kicked out of the Brunswick House. It took some doing to get kicked out of the Brunswick House. We also got kicked out of Malloney's and Club 22. We used to get pretty exuberant. "Hey, good to see you." "How you been?" "What's new?" It turns out we're both on the wagon. We talk real estate, property values. Garage sales are sort of a hobby with him, but nothing catches his fancy here. We say good-bye and I start folding the tent.

Ordinary guys

The major theme in movies these days is ordinary people. There was a movie called just that, *Ordinary People*. It was about how ordinary people faced a big crisis in their lives. Then there's this new one – what is it called? – with Robert Duvall in it. Just about anything Robert Duvall is in lately is about ordinary people facing a big crisis in their lives. They gave him an Academy Award for it. That's how highly people think of ordinary people.

That's great for ordinary people. What about ordinary guys? Nobody makes movies about ordinary guys. You never read about them in the paper. Morley Safer never interviews them. Most ordinary guys are pretty seriously underfunded, but the government doesn't seem the least bit interested in pitching in to provide them with a, you know, an infrastructure.

Nobody ever stopped to think that just because an ordinary guy doesn't have a big crisis in his life that he likes it that way. Some nights when there's nothing on television there's nothing an ordinary guy would appreciate as much as a big crisis. Maybe he wouldn't face up to it if one came along, but what business is that of yours? You can't start discriminating. You can't start handing out crises only to people who you know will face up to them.

What's an ordinary guy got going for him, anyway? Look at his shirts. He doesn't have any clean shirts. That's the way things go for him. Either his shirts are dirty and are piled on the floor of his closet or they are at the cleaners. There's no in-between. Ordinary guys are suspended helplessly between powerful extremes when it comes to shirts.

Then there's beer. It is a strange fact that an ordinary guy is always out of beer. He can go to the beer store and get a two-four and bring it home and feel that thrill of accomplishment that ordinary guys feel when they have fended for themselves, but then one night when he goes to the fridge to get one, they're all gone. All he's left with is a case of empties. This is a big mystery in ordinary guys' lives. Don't think it's easy living a life full of inexplicable things like that.

Speaking of ordinary guys' fridges, take a look in one. All he's got in it is marmalade and mustard and ketchup and a bottle of pickles and some real old milk. Also Worcestershire sauce and Tabasco. Mainly condiments. You get the picture? There's no what you'd call food in there.

Okay, so maybe there's deprivation out there in the Third World and maybe it's no laughing matter, but you try and see how long you survive on a diet of nothing but condiments. No wonder ordinary guys have no colour in their cheeks. No wonder their bellies bulge out.

Ordinary guys don't get much fresh air either on account of somebody painted their windows shut. For fresh air an ordinary guy pretty much has to depend on the television to show him pictures of it on *Wide World of Sports* or when the ball game is on. That's hardly health-giving.

Ordinary guys have been more than a little interested in this whole sexual revolution thing and feminism, all that stuff women have been making such a noise about. Germaine Greer came along and said women should do it whenever they wanted, then a few years later she comes along again and says they shouldn't do it at all. What interested ordinary guys was that all this didn't apply to them. If all these women were doing it, or not doing it, it hardly mattered because, whichever, it wasn't with ordinary guys.

Ordinary guys got no action before the sexual revolution, they didn't get any when it was in full cry, and they're not getting any now that it's over. That about sums it up. No wonder ordinary guys get the feeling that some of the big issues of the age pass them right by.

Sometimes ordinary guys think they should go over to the store and buy a copy of *Penthouse* and a loaf of bread and some cheese slices. This would give them the rudiments of something like a life. But when they look outside it's raining and they're in their stocking feet. Even the elements conspire against ordinary guys.

Long live Brussels sprouts

"Look at this!" Dr. R. Townsend Beggs, activist, scientist, lecturer, author of the bestseller *Wheaties, Breakfast of Villains*, brandished a loaf of bread, brown, sliced, wrapped in a plastic wrapper. "Do you know what this is?" It was a rhetorical question. The crowd shifted on its feet, muttered sullenly.

"Dead wheat!" cried Beggs. "Dead wheat!" cried the crowd in response. It began to repeat the phrase rhythmically. "Dead wheat! Dead wheat!"

"And what do you see in there?" Beggs shouted, pointing through the window of the bakeshop they were assembled in front of. On a tray inside was a stack of croissants. "Dead wheat! Dead wheat!" chanted the crowd.

They pressed forward against the window. The door burst open. Hands were reaching for the croissants as the police arrived. Beggs was arrested and charged with inciting a mob to liberate baked goods. He became the first martyr of what was regarded as Phase Two of the Green Revolution.

Phase One, centred principally in Europe, had to do with efforts to save trees. Phase Two developed from efforts to talk to them.

The idea that plants represented intelligent life, with hopes and dreams, with fears and hurts, had wide repercussions. Soon protests were launched against lumber companies. People who lived in wood houses, even if the wood was only used for trim or porch steps, were often subject to public abuse.

Publishers became haunted men, vilified, reviled, as green revolutionaries broadcast tallies of the arboreal holocaust that had contributed to however many books, magazines, editions of the paper came out that day.

Young people were often the most vigorous supporters of the new order once they realized that all plant life was sacred and they no longer had to eat their vegetables. "Long live Brussels sprouts," became a rallying cry.

People dressed in cotton clothes were spattered with offal. People cutting their lawns were called names for being unkind to grass.

Look on the fate of living things and despair, said the protesters. Our green brothers and sisters are picked, plucked, chopped, and sawn, lopped, topped, cut, mowed down, sliced, diced, mashed, and grated. Grain is rolled, cracked, ground, pounded, shredded, and some of it is even shot from guns.

Action squads were deployed everywhere. When people tried to pick raspberries they were pestered. When they tried to weed their gardens they were harassed. When they measured out flour to make dough to make rhubarb pie they found themselves embroiled in a rhubarb of another sort entirely.

The nation came to realize how much of its lifeblood flowed green and if it stopped flowing there wasn't an industry – from construction to farming to ladling out spaghetti – that was safe. Injunctions were issued forbidding activists to come within 300 feet of green, growing things.

What was more important, economists asked, the health of the nation or the feelings of a lettuce? The revolutionaries responded by asking the rest of the world to boycott Canadian goods as long as a single niblet remained at risk on a Dominion store shelf.

It wasn't an easy time for true inter-species advocates who had already given up eating meat and wearing anything derived from an animal or a fish. They found they had nothing but earnest intentions to sustain them. They grew thin.

One day a green revolutionary of particular sensitivity looked up from his empty plate and said, "What about plates?" Clay was scraped from the earth and put through the fire to make plates. Weren't they friends of the earth? "What about forks?" Didn't ore have feelings, didn't clay, didn't dirt? "How would you like it if you were a rock and you were crushed to make this?" he asked, pounding the sidewalk. That was the start of Phase Three.

Waving farewell

A story on the front page the other day said Canadian National Railways and CP Rail are looking to get rid of the caboose. When a columnist learns of the passing of something such as the caboose it is his bounden duty to wax eloquent on it.

A few years ago North American car manufacturers decided they weren't going to make convertibles any more and columnists waxed eloquent up and down the pike about the passing of the convertible. Now there is a lot of eloquent waxing on the anniversary of D-Day, which was the beginning of the end for Double-U Double-U Two.

But, you may have noticed, after having passed, the convertible has been born again and, despite the events that followed on the Normandy invasion's brave heels, war is back and as popular as it ever was, maybe more. So when we wax eloquent on the passing of the caboose it doesn't necessarily mean that the caboose is about to vanish forever.

(Waxing eloquent on the passing of things is an imperfect science. No matter how often we wax eloquent on the passing of common decency and the old-fashioned values, they seem to keep coming back. How else can you account for the fact that they keep disappearing?)

The railways want to replace the caboose with a black box. Black boxes seem to preoccupy the transportation industry. Once I was on a flight from Yellowknife to Edmonton when the pilot came on the blower and assured us that he, and not some black box, was guiding us across the heavens. He told this story:

"A chicken and a pig were out for a walk when they saw a sign asking for contributions to the church supper. Said the chicken to the pig: 'I'll bring some eggs and you bring a ham.' 'Wait,' said the pig. 'For you to bring eggs, that's a contribution. For me to bring a ham – that's a commitment.'"

The pilot said that if a black box were flying the plane, the airline would be making no more than a contribution to our safety. But with him at the wheel, he and the company were making a commitment. (Sometimes I think the responsibility of having all that silver hair does funny things to pilots' minds.)

Anyway, a friend of mine, a pilot, was on the flight deck of a Canadian airline's brand new Boeing 767 when it was coming in to Calgary. Everything in the cockpit was computerized. The captain said, "You wanna see what this baby can do?" and punched some buttons and the loaded airliner began its descent and landed and braked without anyone ever once touching a single control. It was no-hands all the way.

So don't fool yourself that the black box isn't up there. Soon the pilot's task will be simply to monitor it. Presumably someone will monitor the black box that replaces the caboose, too.

It should have come as a surprise that there is even a need for a black box at the tail-end of a freight, but it didn't. In my romantic days as a waver-at-trains I thought the caboose had no purpose beyond carrying men to sit in the cupola to wave back at people like me who were going not nearly so far and not nearly so fast and who disappeared from sight at the next big bend, clickety-clack.

But age dilutes innocence. In time I learned that those lordly men rocking behind the high windows weren't simply lounging up there, taking in the scenery. They were working. They were watching the track behind to see that no rails had been dislodged by their passage.

How mundane, I thought. Then they got windshield wipers up there. Then the chimney disappeared; the woodstove was replaced with a microwave oven. Then the new cabooses didn't have cupolas at all. That's when I gave up waving at them.

But now when I think of a black box back there doing the watching I wonder if maybe I wasn't hasty. In any endeavour there's no shortage of people looking ahead. But of the people who spend time looking backward, they always seem to be either too sentimental or too critical for my taste. We don't seem to appreciate the simple benefits of looking back constructively and humanely.

That's what those trainmen did, swaying up there in the caboose. They made sure the way was left safe for those coming after them.

Tying the knot

Forgotten how to tie your tie?

While putting on a necktie for the first time in a number of years, and discovering, though my recall is so faulty it can't recall how many joules there are in a kilopascal, that I still remember how to tie it, it occurred to me that there are probably others who haven't worn neckties in a number of years, having adopted a casual style of dress in keeping with a casual age, but who now wish to appear presentable in the period of elegance which we are entering only to discover they don't remember how to tie their neckties.

Here are *10 Steps to Tying a Necktie.*

After selecting a tie and placing it around your neck you must designate the ends. If you designate the large end A, then the small end will be designated B. If, on the other hand, you designate the small end A, then the large end will be B. These instructions are written according to the designations, large A, small B. If, however, you prefer the designation large B, small A, merely begin reading these instructions from the bottom and follow them, in ascending order, to the top.

CAUTION: Do not miss a step. Should accident or injury result from missing a step, the editors will not be held responsible.

Step 1. While holding end B, flip end A up and over and around and under and back and forth and up and under a number of times. (See diagram.) Then thread end B up and back and under and around and in and through as much as seems expedient. At this point you must deal with end C which, although neither small nor large, though possibly smaller or larger than A or B, has called from the airport and wants to drop by. This, and subsequent ends, D, E, and F-sharp must be dealt with summarily.

The classic pattern (plot this on a chart; soap and the bathroom mirror are excellent chart-making materials) will then emerge: a sine curve where the horizontal axis represents sales volume and the vertical axis represents root-crop production.

Step 2. Affix end A to a stationary object. The dresser top is ideal. It can be affixed with a thumbtack, although a railroad spike assures a more lasting bond and some authorities (Solzhenitsyn, *The Gulag Archipelago*, Vol.IV, *Looking Good in Rudnik*) recommend having your ties lined with metal that can be welded to the bars of your cell. This seems excessive. Having affixed end A, draw back as far as you can. Try to avoid cutting off the supply of air to your lungs. When you black out, you have passed the optimum.

Step 3. Draw back slightly less far.

Step 4. Take end B in your teeth. Take end C in one hand and end D in the other, where appropriate. The other ends must be abandoned to fend for themselves. Sorry, but this is a cruel world and sometimes the few must be sacrificed so the many might survive ("The Playboy Advisor," September 17, 1963, *et seq*.). Now writhe all around.

Step 5. The sounds of violent struggle will attract the attention of neighbours who will either come to your assistance (Luke 10:33) or alert the Emergency Task Force (Dial 911). Make sure the door of your residence is unlocked so they can gain entry.

Step 6. It is often a good idea at this stage to take a short rest. An ocean cruise is pleasant if it is within your means (Janus Travel, 1489 Danforth Avenue. See listing in the Yellow Pages). If it is not, treat yourself to a stiff drink.

Step 7. And maybe a snack.

Step 8. When help arrives, explain that your dresser slips when you draw back and needs to be anchored. Have them tie a rope to it which can be fed out the window and attached to the bumper of a truck (See diagram, page 3), or through a series of pulleys to the backs of the proletariat (See diagram, page 59, *Das Kapital*).

Step 9. Put your left arm under your right knee and your right foot in your left armpit and tuck your head behind both elbows (See diagram, page 121, *The Kama Sutra*) ensuring that at all times tab A goes in slot A or its equivalent. If there are any loose wires, they should be connected to the circuit breaker on the main transformer.

Step 10. There. You've tied it. But are the ends even?

The owl in the cemetery

On a number of mornings in the last couple of weeks I have been able to find a great horned owl in Mount Pleasant Cemetery by following the commotion. The commotion is set up by blue jays, and occasionally joined in by crows, engaged in what is called "mobbing." They are pestering – darting at, pecking at, flapping at, screaming at – the owl in the hopes of persuading it to go elsewhere.

About the easiest way to find an owl is to listen for the hysterical sounds of mobbing and then to follow the gang. You will usually find the owl up a tree at the centre of the controversy, trying to look inconspicuous. This isn't easy, especially if it's a great horned owl, which stands about knee-high, has enormous, upright cat's ears, eyes like high beams approaching in a tunnel, and a wingspread that can run to five feet. When a great horned owl swoops overhead, you reflexively duck – it is as if a 747 had come gliding through the trees.

The mobbing business is instinctive. Somehow evolution concluded that if the little birds could drive the intruder away during the day, there was a better chance of the little birds and their broods surviving the night. Night is the domain of the great horned owl, a powerful, efficient, and terrifying killer that comes on silent wings in the darkest hours. Sometimes when the owl strikes its prey dies of fright.

Beneath the trees, a crew is clearing the cemetery of leaves. Hardly a rake can be seen. Rakes are out of fashion. Blowers drive the leaves in little spinning gales toward piles on the driveways. One enormous blower, mounted on the back of a tractor, makes a bellowing moan that ululates like the dying cry of the Tyrannosaurus Rex in a Japanese monster movie.

Between the shrieking birds and the roaring machine, there is a lively racket in the cemetery these mornings.

I allow myself to take my constitutional there only as long as I promise not to get morbid. I carry with me the words of John Muir, the legendary American wilderness traveller, written perhaps a century ago:

"On no subject are our ideas more warped and pitiable than on death. Instead of the sympathy, the friendly union, of life and death so apparent in Nature, we are taught that death is an accident, a deplorable punishment for the oldest sin, the archenemy of life. . . . But let children walk with Nature, let them see the beautiful blendings and communions of death and life, their joyous inseperable unity, as taught in woods and meadows, plains and mountains and streams of our blessed star, and they will learn that death is stingless indeed, and *as beautiful as life, and that the grave has no victory, for it never fights. All is divine harmony."*

I'm not that sold on it. I just don't want to get morbid.

Some of the graves are enchanting. Masseys lie in a miniature Highland castle, part Sir Walter Scott, part Morgan Le Fay. The Eatons have an enormous pillared Grecian mausoleum, its entrances guarded by a pair of bronze lions, green with years. On nights when the moon is full and I am hungry for company, drink has guided me over the cemetery fence to sit with these lions and explain to them all manner of vital things. The lions are a good audience, and interrupt hardly at all.

The epitaphs on the gravestones, when there are epitaphs, and there most often aren't, seem to me very Canadian; cold, as if selected from a book of suitable epitaphs in the monument dealer's office. There is no humour, no cockiness, not a hint of pungency.

"We shall meet again when the day breaks." "To live in the hearts of those we loved is not to die." "Gone but not forgotten." "What we call death is life."

It is like being commended to eternity with the sentiments of a Hallmark greeting card. "Come dear children to my tomb / And see thy mother's peaceful home / Where you shall to your mother come / When all the toils of life are done." Why is it all so Vale-of-Tearsish?

How much better to read, "Having a Hell of a time, wish you were here." Or, "Good riddance." Or, "There's been a terrible mistake."

In the sky, all mourning tones, I saw that November was sliding out of sight. It had been a good month for walking in the cemetery – it had taken care of the morbidity itself. I could just go along for the stroll.